And Then the Roof Caved In

And Then the Roof Caved In

How Wall Street's Greed and Stupidity Brought Capitalism to Its Knees

David Faber

WILEY

John Wiley & Sons, Inc.

Published by John Wiley & Sons, Inc., Hoboken, New Jersey.
Published simultaneously in Canada.

For general information on our other products and services or for technical support, please contact our Customer Care Department within the United States at (800) 762-2974, outside the United States at (317) 572-3993 or fax (317) 572-4002.

Wiley also publishes its books in a variety of electronic formats. Some content that appears in print may not be available in electronic books. For more information about Wiley products, visit our web site at www.wiley.com.

Library of Congress Cataloging-in-Publication Data:

Faber, David, 1964–
    And then the roof caved in : how Wall Street's greed and stupidity brought capitalism to its knees / David Faber.
      p. cm.
    Includes bibliographical references and index.
    ISBN 978-0-470-47423-5 (cloth)
      1. Real estate investment—United States.   2. Financial crises—United States.   3. Foreclosure—United States.   4. Mortgage loans—United States.   I. Title.
  HD225.F23   2009
  332.63'240973—dc22

Printed in the United States of America.

10 9 8 7 6 5 4 3 2

To
Jonathan and Emily

Contents

Acknowledgments

This book is the product of my reporting about the financial crisis that has gripped the world over the past three years. It owes much of its content to the interviews I conducted on camera and off, for the CNBC documentary *House of Cards*, which first aired on that network in February 2009. The producer of *House of Cards*, James Jacoby, spent a year assembling and shaping its contents into a great piece of journalism. Without his work, this book would not have been written. Intelligent, creative, and warmhearted, James is a good friend to whom I am deeply grateful.

Documentaries are collaborative efforts, and as such, *House of Cards* owes its existence to a small group of wonderfully talented people to whom I am indebted. Jill Landes was its co-producer, a TV veteran to whom we would turn time and again to help us navigate a difficult and complex story. I am grateful for her work.

My deepest thanks go to my longtime video editor, the wonderfully talented Patrick Ahearn. Josh Howard is a great friend who, as head of our unit, thankfully gave us the go-ahead to produce *House of Cards* and helped guide us as we made it a reality. He also helped me come up with the title for this book. I was amazingly lucky to have

Mitch Weitzner take over from where Josh left off. Mitch's insights helped make *House of Cards*, and thus this book, far better. My thanks go also to CNBC's management: Mark Hoffman, its president, and Jonathan Wald, who ran business news while *House of Cards* was in production.

Finally, I must acknowledge the wonderful work of my "daytime" producer, Mary Catherine Wellons, who kept me focused on my daily reporting on the crisis for CNBC, while I was also working on our documentary and this book. She's a first-class person with a great mind and a great future.

The story in this book gains its power from the personal experiences related to me by those who were on the frontlines of the mortgage industry and Wall Street. Many of those people would not speak to me on the record, let alone on camera, and so I am especially grateful to the people who chose to do interviews. My thanks go to Michael Francis, Lou Pacific, Bill Dallas, Sylvain Raynes, Ann Rutledge, and Ira Wagner for taking on the tough questions about what they did and why they did it. My thanks as well to the many homeowners who spoke with us, including Arturo Trevilla and Ernesto and Trina Contreras.

Alan Greenspan gave generously of his time during a 90-minute interview that I will long remember. FDIC Chair Sheila Bair was forthcoming and full of insight. I am grateful to them both.

Kyle Bass has tutored me for the past three years in the scary science of subprime mortgages and CDOs. His deep understanding of those subjects helped inform this book. My thanks also go to Jimmy Frischling for aiding in my understanding of all manner of CDOs and securitized mortgage products.

Scott Waxman is unrelenting, a good quality for a book agent. He is also a great supporter. This book would not have happened without him and I'm very happy to have him in my corner. The team at John Wiley & Sons has been nothing short of excellent. I'm proud to be published by a company whose first love is books about business.

My friend, Wendy Flanagan, a much better writer than I, took the time to read my manuscript and assure me it all made sense. My deepest thanks to her. My thanks as well to all my friends for their constant support.

My love to my mom and dad and my entire extended family for their concern, support, and attention. I needed all of it.

The central person in my life is my wife, Jenny. She is my everything, including my first-line editor. During the many weekends when I wrote, she spirited our children out of the house for the day. That's not always easy, even with the two greatest children in history. I like to believe they think it commonplace for a dad to be staying up nights and working weekends to write a book. I'm sure that one day, if they choose to, they'll do a far better job than I. I'm only glad that I have my weekends back to be with them. Nothing could be better than that.

D. F.

And Then the Roof Caved In

Prologue

"On the Verge"

I t's September 14, 2008, the second week of the NFL season. After being out for the day, I've returned home with my family and am hoping to settle into the couch to enjoy the day's late game. But I know that's probably not going to happen. Try as I might to convince myself otherwise, this Sunday is far from typical. Ever since I left the office on Friday, I had been nervously awaiting this moment, when I could begin to make phone calls to try to find out whether the financial world that I have covered for the last 22 years is a thing of the past.

When I left my office at CNBC's headquarters on Friday, it was clear the storied investment bank Lehman Brothers was in deep trouble. I had been reporting on its worsening plight for months. Lehman had been battling a crisis of confidence that began in the earliest days of the credit meltdown. A financial company such as Lehman, which is exchanging vast sums of money every minute with other financial companies, must maintain the trust of those with whom it does business. The minute that trust disappears, as it did earlier in the year with Lehman's competitor Bear Stearns, the firm is unable to meet its obligations. In other words, it's lights out. The concern among investors and, most importantly, the firms with whom it did business, was that Lehman was not being honest about the value of the assets on its balance sheet.

1

The firm had played big in the mortgage industry and many did not believe Lehman's endless claims that it was marking its real estate–related assets at their appropriate value.

There had been plenty of days over the last year when Lehman was free of the rumors and doubt that would color its future. But, like a cancer that retreats into submission, yet still lurks within, Lehman had never been able to fully shake the concerns about its balance sheet. For Lehman, the last few weeks had seen the cancer return with a vengeance, and, as I left work late on Friday, it seemed certain the 114-year-old investment bank would be sold. If a sale couldn't be arranged, it was far from clear that Lehman could keep operating. That would mean only one thing: bankruptcy.

I pulled the phone to my lap, but still kept the football game on, somehow hoping it would all blow over. As I began to review my list of contacts to determine whom to call, my mind went back to a meeting I had with Lehman's chairman and CEO Richard Fuld only three months earlier. I had not seen Fuld for years and we both agreed it might be a good time to get reacquainted. And so, late one June afternoon, I headed to Fuld's office in midtown Manhattan to try to get a better understanding of what was truly going on at the firm he had led for the previous 14 years. A day earlier, the firm had reported a second-quarter loss of $2.8 billion and said it was raising $6 billion in new capital. Lehman was certainly not in good shape, but it seemed poised to survive.

Fuld did most of the talking. He seemed to be testing out a new approach to explaining why his firm was going to thrive in the years ahead. I sat respectfully as he droned on, talking about Lehman's global franchise and all the ways it could make money beyond the financing of real estate. Fuld is a tough guy. But as I sat back and listened to him pontificate on the merits of the firm he had shaped, he seemed out of touch, as though he were not fully entrenched in the new reality of the financial world: a reality in which every firm had become suspect.

Toward the end of our meeting I asked Fuld why he went ahead with a $22 billion deal to finance and buy the giant real estate investment trust Archstone, a deal that compounded its holdings of real estate. It was a deal Lehman could have exited. Whereas doing so would have hurt the firm's reputation, it would have saved it billions in potential losses in what was already an uncertain real estate market. Exiting the Archstone deal would have also saved Lehman from endless conjecture on just how much money it was losing from the deal—conjecture that contributed to a lack of confidence in the firm's solvency. Fuld seemed surprised at the question. "It was a good deal," he told me. "We still think it's a good deal." I really thought the question might prompt a bit of self-reflection or even self-criticism. But that was Dick Fuld. He *believed*. Two days after our meeting, Fuld would fire his longtime number two, Joe Gregory, and his chief financial officer, Erin Callan.

A few quick calls had me now somewhat up to speed with what was developing. Lehman had been having conversations with both Bank of America and Barclay's about an acquisition, but as the weekend came to a close there was no deal. The key reason was that the U.S. government was making it clear it would not step in to take on any of Lehman's bad assets. Without a government assist, would-be buyers were leery. What had seemed improbable on Friday and inconceivable during my meeting with Fuld only a few months earlier, was now likely: Lehman Brothers was about to go bankrupt.

It was only the start of the longest night of my career.

For weeks prior to that Sunday evening, I had also been following the startling decline of another company that was far less visible than Lehman Brothers, but far more important to the health of the world's financial system. American International Group (AIG) was the world's largest insurance company. It was built by a man named Maurice Greenberg into the greatest single powerhouse the insurance industry had ever known. In many countries around the world, Greenberg had written the laws that would govern the sale and use of insurance. AIG was for many years among the most valuable financial companies in the country. Its market value was routinely above $150 billion. But in 2006, the then 81-year-old Greenberg had been forced from the company after New York's Attorney General Eliot Spitzer accused him of wrongdoing. AIG would never be the same. Many of the risks the company took on during Greenberg's reign were risks that he alone may have fully understood. Still, there were few who had any true concern about its financial health.

As a reporter, you tend to follow your sources. While the world was chasing the rapid decline of Lehman, I found myself far more interested in what was going on at AIG. That was because a handful of people I have known for years were involved with the company's travails. AIG had suffered from a series of quarterly losses. Its stock had sunk dramatically. And in the weeks leading up to that Sunday night, it had lost $50 billion in market value. Still, while the idea that Lehman Brothers could go bankrupt had been contemplated by the many investors and trading counterparties that relied on it, few if any of those same constituencies would ever have thought about such a fate befalling the massive AIG.

It was a call that same night that I'll never forget. The voice on the other end of the phone was calm. I was calling to get some insight into any of the night's developing stories and hoped this source might be able to provide it. I remembered this person had done work for AIG and asked whether there was any concern at the insurer about what might happen with a Lehman bankruptcy.

"That's not their concern," was the reply.

"Why not?" I asked.

"Because they are on the verge themselves."

I thought I must have misheard. "On the verge of what?"

"What do you think?"

Yep, it was going to be a very long night.

AIG, which ran a group of highly regulated insurance businesses, was connected to virtually every financial instrument known to the modern financial system through a separate group of unregulated businesses. For many years, the company had the highest credit rating a company could obtain (AAA) and was able to borrow at costs that were not much higher than the federal government. With what was an almost-unlimited supply of cheap money, AIG had done a lot of stupid things. The stupidest of all was its decision to move aggressively into the market for credit default swaps (CDSs).

In AIG's defense, a *credit default swap* is a form of insurance. It gives the buyer of the CDS insurance against the risk of default on any given debt instrument, whether it be a corporate bond, an auto loan, or, to AIG's lasting regret, a subprime mortgage. Credit default swaps trade based on the likelihood that whatever it is they are insuring will default. The greater the chance investors believe there is that a default will occur, the higher the price of the credit default swap. Like so many other businesses on Wall Street, the CDS market made a great deal of sense before it spun out of control. We'll talk more about this phenomenon in Chapter 7, but suffice to say that AIG did not appropriately gauge the risk of all the credit default swaps it was writing.

I made more calls. I spoke to another longtime source who knew what was going on at the company. He told me that on Friday, AIG had been unable to roll its commercial paper. It was an off-the-record comment, meaning that I could not use it in my reporting, but it helped me understand just how bad the situation at the company had become. The commercial paper market is used by what are typically high-credit-quality corporations for their short-term borrowing needs. In that market, corporations can borrow billions of dollars for 30, 60, or 90 days, and, when those debts come due, most corporations simply roll them over for another 30-, 60-, or 90-day term. The problem comes when no one wants to buy a corporation's commercial paper and it is unable to roll. Now I understood how AIG could be "on the verge." Unable to borrow in the commercial paper markets, the company was rapidly running out of money.

It seemed like a good time to call the office. The typical Sunday at CNBC is pretty quiet, given the network does not feature live programming on the weekends. While we have a handful of people on the assignment desk and a few producers working on the next morning's shows, our cavernous headquarters is a lonely place on a Sunday night. Not on this night; it was all hands on deck, and, having not checked in thus far, I was only now made aware that we were going live beginning at 8 P.M. Reporting from my couch with the football game on in the background was no longer an option. I showered, put on a suit, and headed for work.

By 6 P.M., news was starting to pour in on a variety of fronts. The *Wall Street Journal* and *New York Times* were reporting the stunning news that Lehman would be filing bankruptcy, having been unable to convince the Federal Reserve or Treasury to come to its aid. And in a story I had completely missed, it seemed Bank of America had quickly moved on from its brief courtship with Lehman and was very close to buying the nation's largest and most important brokerage house,

Merrill Lynch. Merrill, I would subsequently learn, was fearful that a Lehman bankruptcy would assure it the same fate and chose to save itself with a hastily crafted deal at a mystifyingly high price.

The Lehman and Merrill stories were being well covered by our own reporters and our competitors, so I focused on AIG. I leaned back at my desk and took a deep breath before embarking on another round of phone calls. I had been a financial reporter for two decades. I had covered the fall of Drexel Burnham Lambert in 1989. I had reported on the collapse of the savings and loan industry in 1990. I'd been lucky enough to break the news of the fall of the hedge fund Long Term Capital Management in 1998 and the massive fraud at WorldCom in 2002. I had reported on the tech bubble's inflation in the late 1990s and its bursting in the early 2000s. And here I was, watching three events happening in the same night that taken separately might have been typical of the biggest financial stories of a decade. It was disorienting, to say the least.

In the intricate dance between reporter and source, persistence is the one constant. After speaking with four or five people who each add an insight or level of detail to a report, I usually find it wise to go back to my initial source and try to cajole a bit more information from the person by convincing him or her of how much more I've learned since we first spoke: "I already know this, but could you tell me that one again?" And so, having learned that AIG was desperately trying to raise cash and was talking to private equity firms and Warren Buffett (who controls a huge insurance company), I went back to my original source.

Yes, he told me, AIG was talking to private equity firms and anyone else it thought might be able to lend it money. Its intention was to use certain of its businesses as collateral for a short-term "bridge" loan that it would repay when those businesses were sold. But those talks were not looking promising. AIG needed the money immediately and the firms wanted time to understand its true financial health before committing capital. As a result, my source told me, the company was casting its eyes toward the Federal Reserve. AIG wanted the nation's central bank to give it a bridge loan of $20 billion. But just then, the Federal Reserve and Treasury, which had evidently decided to let Lehman Brothers go bankrupt, were also turning a deaf ear to AIG's pleas.

CNBC broadcast live that evening until midnight. A few moments after we went off air, Merrill Lynch announced it was being acquired by Bank of America. A few hours later, Lehman Brothers filed for bankruptcy. But AIG did not. It wasn't quite out of money yet.

That Monday, a throng of executives from AIG and their many advisors descended on the office of the Federal Reserve Bank of New York. AIG's financial position was getting worse by the minute. Its counterparties reacted to the scary news about its future by pulling their business from the company. That left AIG with even less cash. What was worse, the company's credit rating was going to be downgraded as soon as Monday night, forcing AIG to post more collateral for various transactions. The $20 billion it needed on Sunday night had doubled in less than a day. AIG was now asking for $40 billion.

AIG had a trillion dollars in assets. It did business in every part of the world and it had written credit default swaps on $2.7 trillion worth of debt instruments. While there was debate about whether a bankruptcy filing by Lehman Brothers would devastate the financial system, there were no such arguments about the effect of a bankruptcy for AIG. Among the people whose opinion I have come to trust over my career, the conclusion was unanimous: AIG's failure would cause a systemic breakdown of the financial system given its deep and broad ties into every part of that system. As that Monday evening's telecast came to a close, it looked like the Fed was going to test that conclusion.

Strange things were happening in the credit markets. Confidence, already sorely tested the past 13 months, was all but gone. Financial institutions were severely cutting back on lending to one another in a disturbing pattern that would crest three days later. But still the Fed was not ready to lend AIG money. I had reported on Monday that the investment bank Morgan Stanley and law firm of Wachtel, Lipton had been hired by the Fed to advise it on AIG. It seemed a promising sign for those who were hoping the company would be saved. But as Tuesday began there was no sign that a loan would be forthcoming. That Tuesday morning I reported definitively, based on my conversations with numerous sources who knew, that if AIG did not receive money from the Federal Reserve it would file for bankruptcy the next day.

The Fed blinked. Reluctant as Treasury Secretary Henry Paulson may have been to take the unprecedented step of lending billions of taxpayer dollars to a publicly traded insurance company, the risk of not doing so was too large to take. The Fed's initial recalcitrance had proved costly. What was $20 billion on Sunday and $40 billion on Monday had amazingly become $85 billion by Tuesday night. AIG's business had deteriorated that quickly. The downgrade of its credit rating on Monday night had forced it to post billions in additional collateral. I reported the news that night in what had become our customary breaking news programming. AIG would receive an $85 billion bridge loan from the federal government with a term of two years and an interest rate of LIBOR (London Inter-Bank Offer Rate) plus 8.5 percent. In return for that loan, the federal government would take control of the giant insurer by obtaining 79.9 percent of the company's public shares. The American taxpayer had just bought itself the biggest, most troubled insurance company in the world.

When the credit crisis began in the late summer of 2007, I turned to a group of people I had been speaking with for 20 years to get insight about its significance. I started as a banking reporter in the mid-1980s, and one of the few benefits of growing older is that your sources do, too. The midlevel executives I had spoken with in the 1980s were now running many of our nation's banks. Even in the earliest days of the crisis, when financial institutions were only beginning to show trepidation about extending credit and the stock market was about to hit new all-time highs, my sources were certain that we were in for deep trouble. The investors in the stock market seemed to have no idea what was going on in the credit markets—no idea of how hard it had become to get a loan, even if it was of extremely short duration, and no idea, it seemed to me, of what that fact would mean for our financial markets or our economy.

On Wednesday, after another late night of broadcasting, many people believed that while there was more bad news to come, the worst of the financial tsunami had passed. But those people weren't paying attention to the credit markets. In those markets, panic was setting in.

The credit markets are similar to a sewer system. When they are working well, no one thinks about them. In the same way that we don't question where that clean water that comes out of our tap is actually coming from, most professionals on Wall Street or Main Street don't give much thought to the free flow of credit. It is something we accept as a constant. But when that credit gets backed up, it is reminiscent of a malfunctioning sewage system. People start to notice. And to take the simile one step farther, if a broken sewage system does not get quickly repaired, a host of malicious diseases is not far behind.

A year after my sources had first warned of the deep trouble toward which we were heading, we had found it. Banks that had not been making loans to corporations or consumers were now leery of making loans to each other. The commercial paper market, which had been slowly drying up for a year, was now closed to almost every borrower. And most terrifying of all, fear was starting to spread throughout the system. Every debt security, other than the debt issued by our government, was suspect. People were pulling money out of every conceivable form of debt and pulling their money out of their bank accounts for fear their bank would soon fail.

Panic is not typically rational. But the threat of panic made rational people prepare for the worst, which meant doing the very same things those who were panicking were doing. Money was coming out of everything, including heretofore-safe money market accounts and heading into Treasury bills and bonds. In a reflection of the panic, people were buying three-month Treasury bills that offered no interest rate. They were giving the U.S. government their money and only asking that it be returned to them three months later.

The conversations I began having with my longtime friends and sources (often one and the same) took on a surreal quality. Can you really put money in a mattress? Can I bury gold bullion in my backyard? Should I buy a safe and a gun? What happens when people lose all faith in the currency and it simply becomes a piece of paper? What happens when everyone loses confidence in the creditworthiness of everyone else?

And then, on Thursday morning, September 18, we were face to face with it. Over the past few days, a handful of money market funds had seen vast redemptions that were forcing them to liquidate their holdings. The panic had started when one such fund lost value after it suffered losses from its holdings of debt of the now-bankrupt Lehman Brothers. Some funds were forced to stop their own investors from withdrawing their money immediately, which sowed more panic. The money market funds, typically large buyers of commercial paper, had completely withdrawn from that market. In the same way that AIG had been shut out of the commercial paper market six days earlier, now even corporations without any connection to the financial services business were finding it impossible to borrow. And even banks that had always been happy to lend to each other were no longer willing to do so.

Thirteen months after our crisis in credit began, the United States and the rest of the world were about to watch the financial system implode. Countless corporations would be forced to file bankruptcy. Commercial banks and investment banks, watching their depositors and trading partners exit en masse, would quickly become insolvent.

The word *credit* is derived from the Latin *credere*, which means "to believe." When the belief that you will be paid back disappears, there is no credit. Belief is the lifeblood of a healthy financial system and its disappearance brought the very real possibility that the United States and much of the Western world would be thrown into a financial cataclysm the likes of which we had never seen.

How did we come to this point? How did we lose Bear Stearns in March and Lehman Brothers six months later? How could Merrill Lynch have been forced to sell itself? How did the American taxpayer end up owning AIG? And after all that, how was it that our system itself was still teetering on the edge of collapse? That story begins seven years earlier, in the rubble of the World Trade Center.

Chapter 1

Bubble to Bubble

O n the morning of September 12, 2001, Alan Greenspan, chairman of the Federal Reserve, was hurriedly returning from overseas. No planes were flying into the United States that day, other than his. Before landing in Washington, D.C., Greenspan asked the pilot to fly over the felled towers of the World Trade Center in downtown New York City. As Greenspan viewed the devastation from above, he was deeply concerned about the U.S. economy. Greenspan's overriding fear was that it would simply cease to function. "History has told us that this kind of a shock to an economy tends to unwind it. Because remember, economies are people meeting with each other. And you had nobody engaging in anything. I was very much concerned we were in the throes of something we had never seen before," recalls Greenspan.

When those planes hit the towers, the U.S. was already in a recession. It was a mild recession, to be sure, but a recession all the same. The United States was suffering from the deflation of one of the greatest speculative bubbles our markets had ever seen. It was quite a party while it lasted. Hundreds of billions of dollars had been thrown at technology companies of all kinds in a frenzy that defied all logic and all the tenets of prudent investing. Few thought we would ever see a bubble of its kind again.

The technology bubble was very kind to CNBC. Our ratings were routinely above those of any other cable news network and almost all of our viewers, save those who were short the market, were in a good mood. Each day brought a new high in the NASDAQ, and with each year the suspension of disbelief grew. The years 1997, 1998, 1999, and 2000 were some of the greatest Wall Street has ever experienced. There was a new paradigm in town. Earnings were of little import. The Internet and anything related to it were all a company needed to be focused on to generate enthusiasm. Growth in revenues, regardless of whether that growth came at the expense of actual earnings, was the only thing investors seemed to care about.

The world was awash in capital, which could be raised in copious amounts for even the worst of businesses. This wasn't a bubble, they scolded the nonbelievers, it was a new age. Naysayers were dismissed as "not getting it." I will not rehash all the high points of the great technology bubble of the late 1990s, but for the sake of capturing the flavor of the times, I'll relate some of the more amazing tech-bubble facts.

In January 1999, Yahoo! was valued at 150 years' worth of its expected annual revenues for that year. At that same moment, Yahoo!'s value was equal to 693 years' worth of its expected 1999 earnings. The point is that if Yahoo!'s earnings were to stay the same, it would take 693 years for those earnings to equal what one had spent to buy the stock. That is not really a great value. And Yahoo!, despite being one of the few companies to truly succeed in the Internet era, now trades at 25 times its expected earnings—far below the value it commanded in 1999.

One of the highest-valued mergers of all time involved two companies few people had ever heard of then and most have certainly forgotten by now, JDS Uniphase Corporation and SDL. When JDS Uniphase agreed to buy SDL in July 2000, the deal was valued at $41 billion. The two companies made things that helped fiber-optic networks operate more efficiently, and that was largely the extent of what anyone knew about these companies. JDS Uniphase still exists today. Its stock trades below $5 a share, valuing the company at around $600 million.

Everyone, and I mean *everyone*, seemed to be playing the stock market. Early one morning in the summer of 1998, I parked my car in a spot that blocked a fruit vendor from pulling his cart to his chosen location. The vendor approached my driver's-side window and upon seeing me immediately started singing the praises of CNBC. It seems he sold fruit from his pushcart in the mornings and then returned home to trade stocks for the remainder of the market day. To me, that is the very definition of a bubble.

When it burst, it took a whole lot of money with it and quite a few jobs, as hundreds of dot-com and telecom companies were forced to close their doors when the free flow of capital abruptly ended. By the end of 2000, according to the search firm of Challenger, Gray and Christmas, dot-com companies were cutting jobs at a rate of 11,000 a month. The NASDAQ, which peaked in March 2000 at 5000, fell more than 3,000 points over the next year. With job losses mounting and wealth vanishing, the growth of the economy slowed dramatically through 2000 and stopped entirely by the middle of 2001. And then came 9/11.

Greenspan's Shock and Awe

Alan Greenspan was chairman of the Federal Reserve from August 1987 through February 2006. He was the longest-serving Fed chairman in history, and, until recently, widely regarded as one of the greatest Fed chairmen our country has ever had. He has been endlessly praised for helping to shepherd the economy through the countless shocks it was dealt during his tenure—from the 1987 stock market crash to the collapse of the savings and loan industry in the early 1990s to the implosion of the hedge fund Long Term Capital in 1998 to the horror of 9/11.

Dr. Greenspan's well-worn face shows every one of his 82 years. But he is still sharp of mind and wit. Since the financial crisis hit, Greenspan's legacy has been tarnished. That's one reason why he graciously gave of his time during a September morning in 2008 when I interviewed him at the Mayflower hotel in Washington, D.C.

His celebrity is such that immediately after our interview, his half-eaten bran muffin became a source of focus for our camera crew and my producer, James Jacoby. Our lead cameraman, Marco Mastrorilli, suggested we bag the Greenspan muffin and list it on eBay. Authentication would be relatively easy, since we likely had some film

My Interview with Alan Greenspan
Photo courtesy of CNBC.

Alan Greenspan
Photo courtesy of CNBC.

The Greenspan Muffin
Photo by David Schumacher.

of the man taking a few bites. My producer, however, claimed his father was a great fan of the good doctor Greenspan and asked if he could deliver the muffin to his dad as a gift. We decided that was a worthy home for the Greenspan muffin.

Fed Chairman Alan Greenspan, like every Fed chairman before and since, played the decisive role in figuring out where interest rates in the United States should be set. Whereas investors in the U.S. government bond market can certainly influence longer term interest rates, they take their cue from the short-term rates controlled by the Federal Reserve.

As the bubble in technology stocks inflated, Alan Greenspan kept interest rates in a tight range of between 5 and 6 percent. A couple of months after the NASDAQ peaked in March 2000, rates were raised to 6.5 percent. To put this in perspective, 6.5 percent is a higher rate than we have seen for quite some time, but well below the mid-teens levels at which interest rates hovered in the late 1970s.

It wasn't until the start of 2001 that Greenspan and his Fed governors, seeing a slowdown in the economy, started to lower interest rates. Fed Funds were 6 percent at the beginning of 2001 and, due to seven separate cuts in interest rates, had fallen to 3.5 percent by August of that year. "We did not start cutting rates, in spite of the sharp contraction in the financial system starting in the summer of 2000, until we were sure the dot-com bubble had sufficiently diffused," Greenspan explains.

On the day after the World Trade Center attacks, Greenspan's decision to view the devastation in lower Manhattan was not only about economics, but also about understanding what damage had been done to the payments system relied on by financial companies around the world. Much of the structural backbone of payments resided in lower Manhattan. When a stock was sold, or a bond was bought, or a check was cleared, the processing of those transactions often took place at institutions that were housed in lower Manhattan. And in a true stroke of stupidity, many of the computer systems that backed up those transactions were also housed in lower Manhattan. "There were several institutions which were in serious trouble because their redundancies went down with their primary systems because it was all too close to the World Trade Center," explains the former Fed chairman.

The Fed's first order of business on September 12 was to lend billions of dollars to banks in order to maintain liquidity in the system given the structural breakdowns that had taken place. It was only after the Fed had made sure the process of intermediation for financial transactions would continue to function that it could then focus on what the attacks of 9/11 would mean for the U.S. economy.

Given Greenspan's fear of an economic collapse, it is not a surprise that he aggressively reduced interest rates. The first cut came six days after the attacks bringing the Federal Funds rate to 3 percent. Two weeks later, Greenspan would send rates down another one-half of a percent to 2.5 percent. President George W. Bush went on television exhorting the American people to help keep the economy afloat and go out and shop. The rate cuts kept coming. November 6 saw another one-half percent reduction in interest rates, and the following month Greenspan engineered yet another cut, this time one-quarter of a percent. (See Table 1.1.)

Table 1.1 Interest Rate Cuts Following 9/11

Date	Federal Funds Rate	
	Change	New Level/Range
September 17, 2001	−½	3
October 2, 2001	−½	2½
November 6, 2001	−½	2
December 11, 2001	−¼	1¾
November 6, 2002	−½	1¼
June 25, 2003	−½	1

SOURCE: Board of Governors of the Federal Reserve System, www.federalreserve.gov.

In the space of three months, interest rates were cut in half. Borrowing costs for corporations and consumers had plummeted to a level not seen in almost 50 years. And that cheap money was starting to have its intended effect. Gross Domestic Product (GDP) had fallen sharply in the six weeks that followed the terrorist attacks. But then things began to stabilize. Consumers, whose spending represented 70 percent of the country's economic output, began to spend again.

Long before he became Fed chairman, Alan Greenspan, as a noted economist, had traced the early versions of an important trend he called "mortgage equity withdrawal." In the early 1980s, Greenspan found that when a home was sold, the seller was typically canceling a mortgage that was much smaller than the purchase price of the home. This fact created two outcomes. The person who had sold the home usually increased his personal consumption, meaning he bought more stuff, and the home that was bought from him now had a bigger mortgage on it. Essentially, while the home had changed owners, debt was replacing equity in the home and the cash that was freed up found its way into the cash registers of businesses. Indeed, as a government economist, Greenspan used his "mortgage equity withdrawal" metric to forecast the future sales of cars and other hard goods.

In early 2002, Fed Chairman Alan Greenspan was still following his much-loved indicator of mortgage equity withdrawal, and what he saw gave him some relief that an economic catastrophe had been averted. Unlike the 1980s, when a home was most often sold in order to unlock the equity in it and free it up for spending, by 2002 a vast industry with myriad mortgage products had sprung up, which allowed people to stay in their homes *and* withdraw equity from them. This is known as the *home equity loan*. That loan is essentially a second mortgage in which the debt is backed by the collateral in the home that exceeds the homeowner's first mortgage. While home equity loans had existed for many years, their use became far more widespread during this period because as interest rates fell to historic lows, people could avail themselves of home equity lines of credit at very cheap rates.

But there was another more important trend that was also brought on by the fall in interest rates. People were starting to refinance their mortgages in record numbers. Some people chose to keep their mortgages the same size and simply lower their monthly payments. But many others saw an opportunity to capture equity that had built up in their homes by increasing the size of their mortgage. Because their interest rate would be lower, their monthly payment might not rise at all, while they would find themselves with a slug of cash they could spend on a new car, a new kitchen, a new mink coat, or all three. It was called the *cash-out refinancing* and it would play a prominent role in the collapse that would come six years later.

Greenspan and his cohorts at the Fed quickly noticed the uptick in consumer spending. "You began to see a combination of the personal savings rate declining and mortgage equity extraction rising. And indeed, from a bookkeeping point of view, it was the rising debt that was subtracting from savings. And you could begin to see the impact of that spilling over into consumer markets." Greenspan says it was never the intent of the Fed to galvanize the housing market, but he admits the Fed welcomed the increase in consumer spending. The cuts in interest rates had worked. The increase in consumer spending staved off an economic calamity and was helping to bring the United States out of recession.

The Fed's intent may not have been to galvanize the housing market, but that is exactly what happened. That market, made up of homebuyers, home builders, and the firms that provide them credit, loved low interest rates. While the Fed Funds rate did not dictate the price of a mortgage, which is more closely linked to the rate on a 10-year Treasury bond, it did have a pronounced effect on the price of that 10-year bond. And the Fed kept pushing rates lower; 1.75 percent became 1 percent by June 2003, and Greenspan's Fed kept the Funds rate at 1 percent for a year after that. Our country had never really known 1 percent interest rates. While mortgage rates were nowhere near that level, they were at all-time historic lows.

In 2003, a 30-year mortgage came at an average interest rate of 5.83 percent after having averaged 8.05 percent only three years earlier when interest rates were far higher. In 2004, the average interest rate for the 30-year mortgage was 5.84 percent and in 2005 it was 5.87 percent. The rates for one- and five-year adjustable rate mortgages were also at never-before-seen lows. For example, a one-year adjustable rate mortgage could be secured with an average interest rate of 3.76 percent in 2003. Lower mortgage rates translated into lower monthly payments and that helped make owning a home affordable for many people who had never before contemplated it.

Unbeknown to Greenspan, his interest rate cuts had unleashed an engine of commerce the likes of which our country had never seen. It was an engine fueled by cheap money that would bring the greatest housing boom in history and then devour all it had created and more.

Houses Built on Cow Dung

In 2003, in the Eastvale section of the Southern California town of Corona, Joseph Dunkley, a chiropractor, and his wife, Barbara, a real estate agent, bought a home for a little over $300,000 in a field full of cow dung. The Dunkleys' new home had been built in a field where dairy cows had grazed for decades until the dairymen sold out and moved to central and northern California. The land they left behind smelled terrible. Decades of cow crap will do that to a place. But the Dunkleys and plenty of people like them jumped at the chance to live the American Dream, even if it came with a nasty odor.

The homes built in Eastvale, part of the so-called "Inland Empire," were relatively inexpensive for Southern California and a good deal

Joseph and Barbara Dunkley
Photo courtesy of CNBC.

larger than a home one might find in Orange or Los Angeles county. The developers were building a *sleeper city*, filled with commuters who spent their day working in Los Angeles, but traveled 90 minutes on the choked 91 freeway to spend their nights in their new homes. The Dunkleys were pioneers. "When we moved in I always said you had to have a vision to live here, because there was nothing here. No supermarkets. No retail shopping. Nothing but a lot of cows. And they were just starting to pop up these developments and the people who were developing it were saying 'this is going to be a nice area,'" explains Barbara.

The Dunkleys were undeterred by the commute and the smell and the lack of any real neighborhood. "We had our names on quite a few waiting lists just wanting to buy," said Barbara Dunkley. It took the Dunkleys four months before they had the chance to make a down payment on a home. They did so without even touring a model. "It was so crazy. The lines were huge on the days they would release maybe 15 houses—you'd have fifty to one hundred people in line trying to scoop up the properties," she explained.

The Dunkleys bought their house in January 2003 and moved in that June. In the intervening six months, the value of their house had increased from $300,000 to $400,000, adding $100,000 to their equity before they even pulled into the driveway. The Dunkleys' home was in the first tract of houses to be put up in the new development and all of their neighbors were feeling pretty good. So was Barbara Dunkley. "There was a huge excitement level. People were giddy and we all looked really smart."

Many of the Dunkleys' new neighbors thought they could be even smarter. They began to buy house after house after house in Eastvale, certain that in just a few months' time they could resell those homes at a big profit. It was called *flipping,* and for a growing number of Americans with limitless access to cheap money, flipping became their profession.

A proliferation of new mortgage products, coupled with those low mortgage rates, quickly expanded the population of eligible buyers. The flippers found a willing audience for the homes they were selling and the home builders kept feeding the real estate–starved masses.

In 2002, construction was started on 1.704 million private homes. The next year, the number was 1.847 million. By 2004, construction was starting on 1.95 million new homes, and at the peak of the housing boom in the United States in 2005 there were 2.068 million homes on which construction was beginning. From the Inland Empire of California to the suburbs of Phoenix and Las Vegas to the beach communities of Florida, houses were being built at a torrid pace.

Everyone, says Joe Dunkley, wanted their shot at the American Dream:

The white picket fence. The kids playing in the yard. It's almost cliché, but it's a very real thing for most people. If you have a family, you want a home you can raise your family in. You get caught up in it. And so you see a lot of people might be stretching too far to achieve that because it is within reach, and so you go for it. You swing for the fences and wait for someone to tell you you can't have it. And I don't think around here a lot of people were told no.

During the housing boom of 2003–2006, almost everyone was told yes.

Chapter 2

Home Sweet Home

I n May 2005, Arturo Trevilla, a Mexican immigrant who wanted to be an entrepreneur, bought a house in San Clemente, California for $584,000. It was the first home Trevilla had ever owned and it made him feel like he was finally an equal of his countrymen in the adopted land he called home. "We felt we were part of America because we could afford to buy a house," explains Trevilla.

But Arturo Trevilla could not really afford to buy that house in San Clemente. Trevilla couldn't afford to buy a house anywhere in California in 2005. The mortgage application that Trevilla signed when he was lining up his financing stated he was earning $16,000 a month. The truth was that Trevilla was actually bringing home $3,600 a month.

Trevilla admits he didn't really understand all the terms of the contract he signed. "There were probably more than a hundred pages to sign and only in English. And to be honest, I didn't really understood most of those papers that I sign. Because I was really happy, excited and I totally trust in the people [broker]. I trust them and I just want to get the house."

Trevilla wanted to move his three children to a place where they could play freely. "They can stay for hours playing at the garage and it's really safe, really safe. We can leave our house open during the night and it's really safe."

Arturo Trevilla
Photo courtesy of CNBC.

But he had another motive as well. Trevilla was hoping to start his own embroidery business, but didn't have the capital he needed to get started on his own. His mortgage broker convinced him that the best way to launch an embroidery business was to become a homeowner first. The plan was simple: Trevilla would buy the house and then refinance his mortgage on the house a year later, taking out what he expected would be as much as $70,000 in newly created equity. The 70 grand would be the seed money Trevilla needed to launch his business.

How it came to be that a Mexican immigrant with three children who earned $3,600 a month was able to buy a $584,000 house that he planned to use to bankroll an embroidery business is the story of the subprime mortgage industry.

Opening Doors

Americans have grown up with a pretty strong notion that it's a good thing to own your home. That belief is often emphasized by our political leaders, who treat a rising percentage of homeownership as a key sign that economic times are good. It's no surprise that President Bill Clinton, President George H.W. Bush, President Ronald Reagan, and President Jimmy Carter had each given speeches similar to one delivered June 18, 2002 by President George W. Bush, in which he extolled the virtues of homeownership and exhorted employees of the Department of Housing and Urban Development to help him achieve his administration's goal of increased homeownership, particularly for minorities:

> I believe when somebody owns their own home, they're realizing the American Dream. . . . One of the things that we've got to do is to address problems straight on and deal with them in a way that helps us meet goals. And so I want to talk about a couple of goals and—one goal and a problem. The goal is, everybody who wants to own a home has got a shot at doing so. The problem is we have what we call a homeownership gap in America. Three-quarters of Anglos own their homes, and yet less than 50 percent of African Americans and Hispanics own homes. That ownership gap signals that something might be wrong in the land of plenty. And we need to do something about it. . . . So I've set this goal for the country. We want 5.5 million more homeowners by 2010—million more minority homeowners by 2010. Five-and-a-half million families by 2010 will own a home. That is our goal. It is a realistic goal. But it's going to mean we're going to have to work hard to achieve the goal, all of us.

When you own your home, you are likely to be more involved in your community, more likely to be stable in your employment, and more likely to be creating long-term wealth given the typically slow-but-steady rise in home prices. And, as only Alan Greenspan could put it, "In a market economy which is based on property rights it is very critical to have as broad a swath of people [as possible] who have a vested interest in that system to make it work."

If you were one of those people who wanted the security and stability of owning your own home, the way you would have financed that purchase during most of the postwar era was with a 30-year mortgage at a fixed interest rate. And to get one, you would have had to put down at least 20 percent of the purchase price in cash and fully document many of the financial facts of your life.

The lender would scrutinize your tax returns to make certain that the income you reported was, in fact, the income you made and would review your pay stubs to make sure you were still earning money. Due diligence wouldn't stop there. The loan officer would often visit you at work and go to your bank to verify that you had accounts there. Letters would be written to any finance companies that you might be doing business with to make sure you were current on any payments. Finally, beyond a down payment and verification of income and employment would come questions of character. How many times had you been married? Were you a good neighbor? Were you fair in your dealings? Veterans of the mortgage industry describe the three Cs: *character*, *credit history*, and *collateral*. As a result of all this scrutiny, it would usually take 90 days or more to get a mortgage. Even after the deal was complete, the loan officer would often visit you in your new home just to make sure you were actually living on the premises.

And that is the way it was for a long time. And that is largely why the percentage of the U.S. population that owned their own home typically peaked at around 60 to 65 percent. Beyond that, whether it was because some of us couldn't afford to put up the collateral or because we didn't have a job or had just gotten divorced or liked to move around a lot, there was a group of people who didn't really fit the well-defined parameters for receiving a 30-year mortgage.

Historically, there were also people who were denied the opportunity to get a mortgage because of their ethnicity or geographic location. If you were living in the inner city and were black or Hispanic, even if you had all three Cs, your chance of getting a mortgage that would let you buy your home was slim. But that was something that began to change in the 1970s. Beginning with the Carter Administration, the government made consistent efforts to encourage banks to start offering mortgages to people who didn't typically get them.

In 1977, Congress passed the Community Reinvestment Act (CRA), a bill signed into law by President Jimmy Carter, which for the first time mandated that all banks that received insurance from the Federal Deposit Insurance Corporation (FDIC) be evaluated by their regulator to make sure they were meeting the credit needs of the *entire* community that they served. The CRA didn't have specific penalties for noncompliance and it didn't tell banks to go out and make high-risk loans. But it did lay the groundwork for addressing the then-underserved needs of many minority communities.

In 1980, Congress passed the Depository Deregulatory and Monetary Control Act, which eliminated rate caps for mortgages. The lenders could, if they chose, get paid a higher interest rate for taking on a riskier borrower. Still, in 1980, there were not too many mortgages being extended to borrowers who didn't fit the traditional profile that banks had been using for the previous 40 years. Minority homeownership trailed that of whites by almost two to one.

So Congress kept trying. It strengthened the CRA by making it easier for individuals to monitor whether their bank was living up to its promise to reinvest in the community. In 1993, President Clinton and Treasury Secretary Lloyd Bentsen tried to make it easier for banks to comply with the CRA by making the paperwork that went along with compliance less burdensome. And Congress made it clear it expected banks' regulators to weigh their respective CRA ratings when weighing in on mergers and the like.

Slowly, banks began to lend to groups of people who had previously been unable to gain a mortgage. The early results were encouraging. It turned out that plenty of people who had been shunned for years were perfectly capable of paying back their mortgages, even if that mortgage came at a higher price. That success in turn encouraged other lenders to begin exploring the depths of the credit spectrum, where people with poor credit histories or a lack of some or all of the three Cs lurked. That was when the subprime industry was born.

An Industry Is Born

The subprime industry's lineage is traced back to 1993. Whereas it was the banks, motivated to live up to their CRA obligations, that began what was called *subprime lending*, it was soon taken over by non-bank lenders that were not covered by the Community Reinvestment Act.

Maybe you remember the advertisements for The Money Store, or the slogan for Beneficial Finance, where you were always "good for more." These were among the first subprime lenders that, along with a bunch of now-forgotten consumer finance companies, began to carve out the niche of lending to people who didn't qualify for prime mortgages. Quite a few of these companies went public in the mid-1990s, such as Cityscape Financial, AMRESCO Residential Credit, and FIRSTPLUS Financial Group.

Many of the early subprime loans were refinancings for people who were not minority homebuyers, but rather existing homeowners who were "house poor" and could not find credit elsewhere. The lenders made the loans up to a level of 50 percent of the home's value. They knew that if the person defaulted, there was still a home they could seize and very likely sell for a price above the amount of the loan. The same was true for new subprime mortgages. While the borrower might have bad credit, the bank would lend only up to 60 percent of the home's value, providing it lots of protection in case of default. And of course, all these firms still demanded the same type of verified facts about income and employment that formed the backbone of their decision to extend credit.

The firms, small as they were, did well. The Money Store and Green Tree Financial, another player in subprime lending, found themselves on the receiving end of multibillion-dollar acquisition offers (Green Tree from Conseco Financial and The Money Store from First Union). But even with those relatively high-profile transactions, subprime lending was still considered a backwater, dwarfed as it was by the multitrillion-dollar market for prime mortgages. And toward the end of the 1990s, things got pretty ugly.

It turned out that some of the publicly traded subprime firms had been rather aggressive with their accounting. It didn't help when mortgage rates started climbing in 1998–1999, shutting off their ability to provide home financing that people could afford. The carnage mounted quickly. Restatements of earnings were coupled with poor business conditions and shares in firms such as FIRSTPLUS and AMRESCO plunged. (Both eventually went bankrupt.) And what about those acquisitions of The Money Store and Green Tree Financial? They turned out to be two of the most toxic deals of the decade. First Union eventually shuttered The Money Store and took a $2 billion write-off, while

Green Tree Financial and its aggressive accounting policies helped tip its buyer, Conseco, into a bankruptcy of its own.

By 2000, as George W. Bush began his first term, the subprime industry was on its knees. It had never been more than a minor player in the nation's mortgage market, but during its ascendance it had helped furnish mortgages to people who might not otherwise have qualified for them. And now, most of the major providers of those mortgages were out of business.

With the tech bubble at full inflation and interest rates at multiyear highs, no one was thinking much about a nationwide housing boom in 2000. Subprime mortgage lending was barely an afterthought. The industry nursed its wounds, but the preceding seven years had laid a foundation for the explosion in subprime lending that was to come.

First, those subprime lenders had proved there was a willingness on the part of investors to buy the mortgages they originated. Of no less importance, those subprime pioneers had developed mortgages that deviated greatly from the traditional 30-year fixed-rate product. They created mortgages that were affordable to the client base they were targeting: adjustable-rate mortgages that began with a low rate that adjusted higher, and mortgages with options on what the holder had to pay in a given month. The subprime pioneers still demanded that borrowers document their income and provide a significant down payment on their home. And they offered refinancing when they knew the collateral of the home far exceeded the value of the mortgage. But those boundaries would quickly be overrun in the boom that was to come.

Subprime Returns

Bill Dallas has been in the mortgage business his entire life. You might not think there's much science involved in the process by which mortgages are given out in this country until you've had a chance to talk to Dallas. He can reel off statistics related to every part of the mortgage business going back 30 years, and after talking with him you come away with a deeper appreciation for the intricate relationship between borrower and lender.

Bill Dallas
Photo courtesy of CNBC.

Dallas has founded two mortgage companies. He started First Franklin in 1978. It eventually became a mortgage originator that targeted borrowers who weren't quite subprime, but were certainly not prime, either. It was sold to National City Bank in 1999. A few years after leaving First Franklin, Dallas founded another mortgage company, called Ownit Mortgage Solutions, in 2003, whose brief life was dedicated to serving the same clients that First Franklin had targeted.

Dallas has the trim bearing of an athlete. It seems fitting that his Linkedin page lists his interests as golf, running, working out, weight training, coaching kids, skiing, and fishing. Somehow with all those sports going on, Dallas also finds time to manage the assets of the Olsen twins and help run the Fox Sports Grill chain of restaurants, which he owns with some partners. He's an intense and analytical guy. During a long interview near his base of operations in Southern California, Dallas came back time and again to the metrics he had relied on through his 30-year career in the mortgage business—things like loan-to-value

Bill Dallas with David Faber
Photo courtesy of CNBC.

ratios, credit scores, and historical rates of home price appreciation. Bill Dallas helped build the business of providing mortgages to people with less-than-perfect credit and then he watched it die.

Dallas says the subprime business was near death in 2000, when virtually all the public subprime companies went bankrupt. "My view was that subprime was dead and almost buried. And right before it got buried, we had September Eleventh."

The low interest rates that Alan Greenspan engineered saved the subprime business from oblivion. As mortgage rates moved lower and housing prices started moving higher, people began to use refinancing to take equity out of their homes. The subprime mortgage industry was back. Soon, it would be bigger than anyone could ever have imagined.

Chapter 3

The Subprime Machine

T he center of the subprime mortgage universe in this country is Irvine, California. In one small group of nondescript office complexes, companies that had survived the late 1990s and ones that were just getting their start were housed in such close proximity that everyone knew everyone else's business. And they were all becoming aware that a nationwide boom was taking shape. These lenders, while based in Southern California, would dole out subprime mortgages from coast to coast.

Lou Pacific, a big-armed, straight-talking Vietnam veteran with a resonant voice who fancies Hawaiian shirts and Neil Young songs, has been giving people mortgages for 30 years. Pacific was brokering mortgages when interest rates were 18 percent and he was brokering mortgages when they were 5 percent.

Lou Pacific is a cynical soul, but he wasn't born that way. He's just seen too many people do too many stupid things for it not to leave a mark. And he's seen his share of housing booms, though he admits there's not likely to be anything that ever will compare to what happened in Southern California from 2002 until 2006. We had lunch at what had been the central watering hole for brokers from New Century, a firm that was one of the largest players in the nation's subprime market.

Lou Pacific
Photo courtesy of CNBC.

Pacific began reminiscing:

> As the prices started going up it created more or less a frenzy.
> I literally had clients, friends, family who would call me and say
> they knew somebody who had bought a property with noth-
> ing down, no money at all out of their pocket "and they turned
> around and sold it a week later and made $50,000. How can
> I do that?" And it was just a snowball effect.

Bill Dallas and Lou Pacific grew up in an industry with well-
defined rules. They had both given mortgages to people who didn't
conform to the criteria of a prime borrower. But when they lent
to non-prime borrowers, these veterans still demanded that borrowers document their income and put money down on the home. But
as the housing market began its historic climb upward in 2002, the
rules they had lived by no longer seemed to matter. It's not that Dallas
hadn't given mortgages to people who weren't considered great credits;

**Lou Pacific and I Tour the Empty Office Buildings Once Occupied
with Subprime Lenders**
Photo courtesy of CNBC.

he'd built a business based on it and was in the process of building another. But at his company, Ownit Mortgage Solutions, Dallas's
demand that borrowers fully document their income was quickly
becoming a thing of the past.

Dallas recalls watching the subprime industry rise out of its grave.

> The dead, lifeless body of the mortgage business suddenly gets
> lower rates and the asset class starts to bubble up as home prices
> begin to appreciate. The consumer, who's always late to the
> party, gets a memo that says, you know, rates are low, [and thinks]
> "I should buy." They rush out and suddenly the guidelines
> start to expand. And how do they expand? With no-income-
> verification loans, just state your income. Whatever you make,
> come on in.

The *stated income loan* almost seems like a joke. It means exactly
what it says. Borrowers were able to tell the lender how much money

they earned without the lender being able to verify whether the borrower was telling the truth. How, one might ask, was it possible that people could get a mortgage without the lender knowing how much money they made? Like a lot of good ideas gone bad, the stated income loan was created for a specific borrower. Lou Pacific remembers seeing the product in the mid-1990s, when it was used specifically for self-employed people who couldn't always document their full income: "It was a good product in the beginning, especially out here in Southern California, where there are a lot of self-employed people."

The stated income loan was also a good one for professionals like doctors or lawyers, who had voluminous tax returns that sometimes made it difficult for the lender to ascertain the true amount of cash they had coming in every month. But those buyers who used a stated income loan were forced to cough up a significant cash down payment in addition to having substantial sums of money in verified bank or investment accounts.

Bill Dallas first heard of the stated income loan in 1986, when General Electric Mortgage Insurance created a product called "Easy Docs." "It was created for a jumbo loan, a loan over a certain limit. GE would provide insurance on the mortgage and the borrower could state their income as long as the loan was below 65 percent of the purchase price," Dallas explains.

How times had changed. By 2003, stated income mortgages were being given to people who put up less than 5 percent of the home's purchase price. The litmus test of substantial down payment coupled with verified assets had been done away with. And these mortgages were not just being used to allow people to buy new homes. The vast majority of subprime lending that took place from 2003 until 2007 was not for the purchase of a new home, but to refinance a mortgage on an existing home. It was Greenspan's mortgage equity withdrawal trend writ large and gone haywire.

"Most people, especially in Southern California, especially in Orange County, live off the equity in their houses," explains Lou Pacific. "I have clients who I would refinance every year. And every time I'd do it for them they would pay off all their credit cards and their car loans. The following year, and this is when properties were going through the roof, they would call me up and say they ran their credit cards up again and they need to take another loan out."

The word *subprime* has a pejorative tone. It seems to imply that the people getting these mortgages were less-than-stellar members of the community. But that is really just a fiction. Subprime mortgages were only one part of a broad decline in lending standards that applied to every mortgage that was extended in the United States from 2003 to 2007. The frenzy of creative mortgage products was far from confined to those with bad credit. It extended to borrowers with perfectly good credit as well.

You may have heard of something called an *alt-A* mortgage. It's not a very appealing or descriptive name. It's actually a catchall name for a host of mortgage products that were enthusiastically offered by lenders trying to help people buy homes when their incomes weren't really up to the task. The alt-A mortgage market would ultimately become as big as the subprime market and it was born from the same need. The income of potential buyers was not rising nearly as fast as the prices of the homes they wanted to buy. The *A* in *alt-A* does not stand for *affordability*, but well it should.

A number of creative mortgage products fall under the banner of alt-A, many of which were also used in the subprime section of the market. Four such products are the interest-only, hybrid ARM, negative amortization adjustable rate mortgage, and option ARM:

1. *Interest-only:* This is a mortgage that allows borrowers to make monthly payments for a specified period that cover only the interest due on the mortgage. During that period, the outstanding principal of the mortgage doesn't decline, but after the interest-only period concludes, the monthly payment increases to a level that fully amortizes the loan over its remaining term. That means your payments go up to a level higher than they would have if you'd been paying interest and principal from the start.

2. *Hybrid ARM:* A favorite in the subprime world, this mortgage has an initial fixed interest rate, which converts to an adjustable rate. The *2/28 loan* is an example: It's a 30-year adjustable mortgage that doesn't have its first adjustment until two years have passed. That two-year period is typically at a low, or *teaser* rate, but once the loan adjusts

to an adjustable rate (its rate can change monthly, semiannually, or annually), it usually carries a far higher rate.

3. *Negative amortization adjustable rate mortgage:* This is an adjustable rate mortgage that allows borrowers to fix their payment for at least a year. So if the mortgage is adjusting every month and going higher, the borrower's payment will not. That's a good thing, except for the fact that if the fixed interest payment is not really enough to pay the actual interest and principal, the difference gets added on to the unpaid principal balance to create what is called *negative amortization*. In other words, instead of your mortgage's balance going down, it's going up. Most of these loans have a cap on how much can be added to the principal over the life of the loan.

4. *Option ARM:* This is another adjustable rate mortgage product that gives borrowers various payment options each month. In a typical option ARM, borrowers are allowed to make a minimum payment that is below the amount of interest due on the mortgage. The difference gets added to the mortgage's principal (negative amortization). Borrowers can also choose to make interest-only payments or pay the fully amortizing amount.

Many of these products, while exploding in popularity during the housing boom, had been around for a long time. The option ARM, for example, made great sense for a niche of the market. It was originally targeted toward people in sales and others who relied on commissions. It allowed them to ride out a bad month by choosing the low-payment option and then pay back more of their loan when they had a good month. When it was given to that population, the option ARM had a strong record of low borrower defaults.

By 2005, however, $238 billion of option ARM mortgages were written. It had become an "affordability" product, allowing people to buy homes that their annual income would not realistically allow them to afford.

In 2002, alt-A mortgages accounted for just 5 percent of all mortgages originated. By 2006, one of every five mortgages given out was classified as alt-A. Given that subprime had a similar share of the market, the combined share of subprime and alt-A reached 40 percent of the mortgage market by 2006. And of those alt-A mortgages used for purchasing a new home, a staggering 81 percent were stated income loans.

Of course, those statistics mean that 60 percent of the mortgage market was still considered prime. But in the great housing boom of 2002–2007, *prime* also seemed to have lost its meaning.

Mark Hanson is one of the foremost experts and a 20-year veteran of the California mortgage market, which is the largest mortgage market in the nation. Hanson has probably kept every piece of paper that has ever crossed his desk. When I ask him for information on any type of mortgage that has been written in the past decade, he is able to produce it.

Hanson says he became concerned about the mortgage market back in 2003, not when he saw lending standards fall for subprime or alt-A borrowers, but for prime borrowers. Back then, says Hanson, Wells Fargo was the lender to beat when it came to aggressive rates and mortgage programs.

Hanson recalls a mortgage Wells Fargo rolled out in the middle of 2003 for prime borrowers. It was an adjustable rate mortgage that allowed for interest-only payments. Borrowers would have to fully document their income, but could get a mortgage for up to 95 percent of their home's value. Because the mortgage might start with interest-only rates as low as 4 percent, lots of people with poor credit could qualify. Wells Fargo, according to Hanson, allowed for borrowers with debt-to-income ratios of 50 percent and low credit scores. Despite all that, Wells included this mortgage under its "Prime" loan programs. It quickly became the industry standard.

And that was not the worst of it. Whether subprime, alt-A, or prime borrowers, people were taking on mortgages that often amounted to almost the entire value of the home. It didn't always appear that way. In a report dated March 12, 2007, longtime housing analyst Ivy Zelman, then of Credit Suisse, uncovered the fact that whereas most buyers were reported to be putting down as much as 20 percent of the purchase price of their home, it was far from the truth.

Based on a survey Zelman did of home builders, she found that the average loan-to-value ratio among their customers in 2006 was 91 percent. How did the homebuyers do it? They were taking on *second mortgages*, also known as *piggyback loans*. A piggyback loan would literally do just that—ride on the back of the original mortgage. A popular loan option was for a buyer to take out a first mortgage for 80 percent of the value of the home and then cover the remaining 20 percent, not with a cash down payment, but with a second mortgage that typically carried a higher interest rate. Zelman estimated that roughly half of all the homes purchased in 2006 were at loan-to-value ratios of 95 percent or more, thanks to piggyback loans.

Piggyback loans are a dangerous product for the lender, because they are second in line to the first mortgage if the borrower can't pay and the lender forecloses on the house. That position is known as *having a second lien* on the home. If the value of the house is equal to or less than the value of the first mortgage, the lender on the second mortgage gets nothing. But back in 2003, 2004, and 2005, that was never a concern. Housing prices were shooting ever skyward, so, even in the remote case of having to foreclose, the lenders would be left with a house that had increased in value from the time they granted the mortgage. Would piggyback mortgages ever be thought risky? Never!

In order to understand the new levels of risk lenders were willing to take on, consider the following press release from Bill Dallas's old firm, First Franklin. In June 2004, that company shattered all previous records in its 23-year history by originating $3.56 billion in new, *nonconforming* mortgages. The numbers themselves are stunning enough; one firm originating that kind of volume in one month gives a sense of how many exotic mortgages were being originated in the United States during that year. But my favorite bit of this promotional release comes well after the lead:

> Launched at the end of March 2004 to give borrowers even more financing options within First Franklin's product suite, Stated Plus and RapidRefi began to roll out in the second quarter. Stated Plus offers a new income documentation alternative, giving self-employed, 1099 and salaried borrowers who possess qualifying financial assets the ability to state their monthly income and qualify for more loan options, such as no-down-payment financing. Perfect for homeowners looking to lower their payments, lock in a lower rate quickly or cash out equity, RapidRefi simplifies the refinance process with faster income and mortgage history verification.

Do you see what I mean by haywire? First Franklin, which was among the most respected of mortgage lenders, was pushing a stated income, no-down-payment mortgage, while touting its ability to refinance people rapidly. This was not an ad, but a press release aimed at the financial community. In looking back on this press release, one is struck by the obviousness of it all. Clearly, the idea of underwriting a mortgage to a well-defined and time-tested set of standards was no longer something the industry worried about.

From Delivering Pizza to Delivering Mortgages

To fully understand the level of absurdity to which lending standards fell in the boom years of housing, it's worth an inside look at one of the many short-lived subprime lenders that popped up in the office parks of Irvine, California: Quick Loan Funding.

Quick Loan was founded in 2002 by a Lebanese immigrant named Daniel Sadek. Thanks to some great reporting in the *Orange County Register* by John Gittelsohn, we know that Sadek's formal education ended with the third grade, and that he started out in the United States by pumping gas. He quickly moved on to selling used cars and from there to selling new luxury cars such as Mercedes. It would already be a pretty good immigrant "up-by-his-bootstraps" story if it ended there, but of course it doesn't.

Sadek found that he was selling a lot of Mercedes to young guys who were loan officers at the ever-growing group of mortgage lenders that were sprouting up in Southern California. It seemed like a good business; these guys didn't have much experience and they were clearly making a lot of fast money, so Sadek figured he would give it a try.

It doesn't take much to become a licensed mortgage broker in the state of California. For $250 and the time it would take you to pass the written portion of a motor vehicles test, you can get a California Finance Lender license to sell mortgages from the California Department of Corporations. Sadek paid his money, posted the required bond of $25,000 that's needed to start the business, and passed a quick background check. After that, he could hire anyone he wanted to sell mortgages and they would not be required to pass anything. His salesmen were not required to take a test, have a background check, or receive any training whatsoever.

A few years after he started Quick Loan, with its infamous tag line of "Don't wait, we won't let you," Sadek's firm was financing $200 million worth of mortgages each month and he was taking home as much as $5 million a month in compensation. Quick Loan was far from one of the biggest players in subprime mortgages such as Ameriquest or New Century, which at their height were financing $5 billion a month in mortgages. Still, during the boom years, Quick Loan employed 700 people, one of whom was Lou Pacific.

Pacific met Daniel Sadek in the late 1990s, when he was selling expensive cars. A few years later, in 2004, Pacific would join Quick Loan as a vice president in charge of the firm's real estate division. Quick Loan's business had been almost entirely focused on the refinancing of mortgages up to that point and Pacific was brought in to help the firm originate more purchase mortgages. When he joined, Quick Loan was producing only around five mortgages a month that were for the purchase of a home. Pacific came in and started training the so-called "loan officers" about how to sell a purchase mortgage. Thirty days after his arrival, Pacific says Quick Loan went from funding five purchase mortgages a month to funding a hundred a month. It wasn't because he was *that* good, says Pacific; it was because it was *that* easy:

> The client tells you they're looking to buy a house, but they don't have good credit. They won't be putting money down. And they get excited. There isn't anything you could say to talk them out of it because their friends, their family and their neighbors are all buying property and they're turning around and flipping it and making money.

Once you could generate a lead, closing the mortgage was a cinch. The main lesson Pacific tried to impart to his student loan officers was to keep the client calm:

> It's not even really a sale by our guys; you're just trying to educate them about the terms of the loan. But if they're stating

their income and they're just going to turn around and sell the house anyway, there's not a whole lot of sticker shock with these people.

The terms of the mortgages Quick Loan was selling should have induced sticker shock. Quick Loan was putting people into the most notorious of subprime loans, the *2/28 loan*. For the first two years, the mortgage would carry an interest rate as low as 1.5 percent, but after two years that rate would adjust to as high as 7 or 8 percent and might often remain there for the next 28 years of the mortgage.

Pacific says he knew that few of the people getting these mortgages would ever be able to pay them back. He fully admits that Quick Loan took on the nastiest of subprime loans. It offered mortgages to people with credit ratings below 500, typically referred to as a *sub-500 FICO score*. (*FICO* stands for the Fair Isaac Corporation, which developed this widely used measurement of credit risk in the 1950s.) Quick Loan's nasty mortgages were not just for people with terrible credit, but usually had the borrowers state their income and get a loan that equaled as much as 95 percent of the purchase price. With terms like that, is it any wonder these people might not be able to pay back their mortgage?

Pacific makes no apologies:

> If I hadn't helped them do what they wanted to do, that they were adamant about doing, then somebody else would have done it and somebody else would've taken advantage of 'em rather than me just helping 'em reach their goal. And they would've went somewhere else that would've had somebody who didn't care even a little bit like I did. They were adamant about this. They wanted to buy the house. They wanted to flip it. They wanted to make the money.

Quick Loan's sales force of loan officers were almost as giddy as its clients. They were drawn from the ranks of car salespeople, pizza deliverers, and kids who had worked in electronics stores:

> I mean you're taking a kid who used to sell pizzas, literally, and now he's making $20,000 a month with no training. And the

hardest part I had with them was they would get greedy to the point where they wanted to go out and buy brand-new cars and brand-new homes.

Pacific says he tried to explain the realities of the marketplace to his young charges and their 36-year-old boss Daniel Sadek. "I would say, 'Look, you can get the cars and the houses, anyone can get that. It's *keeping it* that's hard.' But they didn't understand the concept. They had never been through a downturn. I even told Daniel [Sadek], 'Getting it's easy, keeping it's hard.' But he would just laugh," recalls Pacific.

With his business booming, Sadek decided he wanted to move Quick Loan from its somewhat-austere office space to a far grander site, and asked Pacific to find him a new building on which he could place Quick Loan's sign so that it would be seen from the freeway. Pacific warned Sadek that home prices might soon stop going up and Quick Loan's future would be better protected by keeping overhead low. Sadek wasn't interested in that. "He liked the high life and the flash," says Pacific.

Living the Dream

Daniel Sadek is a lover of cars. And with $5 million a month flowing into his own pockets in years like 2004 and 2005, he was able to buy a lot of them, including an Enzo Ferrari and a Saleen S7. Sadek also became a movie producer, featuring his then-fiancée Nadia Bjorlin in a movie he bankrolled to the tune of $26 million. It was called *Redline* and featured fast cars (most of them owned by Sadek) and a plot line that involved an attractive automobile fanatic, also the lead singer for the hottest unsigned band on the West Coast, who finds herself caught up in illegal drag racing competitions organized by exotic car fanatics. I have not seen *Redline*, but I did ask my producer Mary Catherine Wellons to watch the movie and give me her review. Mary Catherine is an educated young woman, an honors graduate of the University of Virginia who frequents many of the cultural offerings of New York City. She said *Redline* may be the worst movie she has ever seen. Online reviews of the movie after its debut in April 2007 indicate that Mary Catherine is not alone in her assessment.

Aside from being awful, *Redline* did have one other claim to fame. During a promotional stunt for the movie, its star, Eddie Griffin, crashed Sadek's million-dollar Enzo Ferrari into a retaining wall.

While Lou Pacific got Quick Loan's production of purchase mortgages humming, Sadek's firm still relied on refinancings for 90 percent of its business. Quick Loan, like almost all of its competitors in the subprime market, used late-night and early morning advertising to drive its business. The ads, which would appeal to people in financial trouble, offered them the help they needed if they called Quick Loan's operators. "It was like watching Disneyland on TV," says Pacific. "If you're the average person watching this, you're thinking, 'That's me. And I don't have to worry about my credit score. I don't have to worry about being late on my mortgage. I can get a loan in a week.'"

When the calls would come in, the call center would put them through to the loan officers who were available at that time. These were the same loan officers who had only recently left their jobs delivering pizza. A conversation that usually lasted 20 to 30 minutes would ensue.

The loan officers were interested in only a few things: how much the caller's home was worth, how big their existing mortgage was, and their credit score. "If there's equity in that home and they have a credit score that's high enough, then they'll do a loan for 'em. They just walk them through the process from there. The main thing the borrowers want to know when they call is, 'How fast can I do this?'" explains Pacific.

The whole process, from that first 20-minute phone call until the check from Quick Loan cleared, could occur in as little as a week. And the borrowers could use their new money to pay off bills, take a vacation, put in a pool, or buy anything else their heart desired.

Diving into Deep Trouble

Ernesto Contreras is familiar with that feeling. Contreras and his wife, Trina, were initially beneficiaries of the housing boom. The couple bought their first home in 2002 for $172,000 and sold it three years later for $405,000. With the profit from the sale, the Contrerases were able to pay off their bills and car loans, and like so many other homeowners

Ernesto and Trina Contreras
Photo courtesy of CNBC.

looking to move up in the world, they used the rest of their windfall to make a down payment on a far bigger home in a new neighborhood. That home cost $500,000 and it didn't take long for Ernesto Contreras, who has worked in the swimming pool industry for the past 15 years, to become concerned that the couple had reached too far.

> It was a little more house than we could probably handle finan-cially. And so when it came to that point where "you know, this is a little much for us, but we want to stay if it's possible," we approached our mortgage broker asking what can we do to try and stay here.

The Contrerases' mortgage broker happily complied with their desires. They were able to refinance with a negative amortizing adjust-able rate mortgage that had payments that were lower than their current mortgage. Even better, the couple was able to extract equity from their new home. They used the cash to put in a pool. "We went into this saying I want to get into a loan that works for us," explains Ernesto. "But then I want to pull money out so I can have that pool. I got three boys and we said, 'You know what, if we're gonna stay, let's have everything and make this the house we really want.'"

The Contrerases loved their new pool, which attracted lots of kids from the neighborhood. But they didn't really understand the mortgage that gave them the money to pay for it. Their new mortgage allowed the Contrerases to make a monthly payment that was below the actual amount of interest they owed. The difference between what they paid and what they owed was added to the principal balance of the mortgage in a process called *negative amortization*. Rather than the outstanding balance of the mortgage declining with each monthly payment, as it would with a traditional mortgage, the Contrerases' mortgage was getting bigger.

"Well, every month getting our mortgage statements, it shows our balance and little by little that balance started creeping up," explains Trina Contreras, "and then the hundreds turn into thousands and another thousand and before you know it, I'm like 'Wow, this is not a good thing.'"

Remember, this mortgage product typically offers one year at a fixed rate that is lower than the actual payment (which is adjusting each month). The Contrerases were having enough trouble keeping up with their mortgage payments *before* the yearlong fixed rate adjusted upward. Having learned too late about the mortgage they had been put into, they now understood their monthly payments would increase by $2,000 when the mortgage adjusted. "We knew that in a couple or three months we're going to get a letter in the mail telling us we can no longer make the small payment and have to move up to the next level. And the next level we can't afford," said Ernesto Contreras. They tried to work with their lender to refinance again, but that door was closed.

"This is our home," explained Trina. "It's not just a house. We've made memories here. My kids are part of the community, not just in school, but in sports. We have a ton of friends. It's not a good feeling knowing, like, what are we gonna do?"

What the Contrerases decided to do was to stop paying their mortgage. "You stop paying and you hope the bank calls you in some desperation to ask, you know, 'let's fix this,'" explains Ernesto Contreras. "The banks already told me they'll do nothing for me and I'm not gonna get a raise tomorrow that pays me a thousand more a month, so it's what I have to do. It may literally come down to me having to walk away from this house and at that point, you know, what do I do? I guess we move into an apartment and start over."

Chapter 4

Eyes Wide Shut

As the frenzy in subprime lending was taking shape, Alan Greenspan was oblivious. It's not that he didn't see signs of a housing boom. "Our extraordinary housing boom cannot continue indefinitely," he warned his colleagues on the Federal Open Market Committee (FOMC) in November 2002. But the boom that Greenspan saw taking shape was, in his mind, a typical housing boom in which prices would advance at too quick a pace and might then fall back a bit, or rise at a far slower rate. "There has always been an uptrend in home prices in the United States, largely because we don't have very much productivity in housing, because we customize our houses, which is anathema to productivity growth. And the history of home prices in the United Sates is that they go down very, very rarely," Greenspan told me.

He says the Fed was monitoring the rise in home prices relative to what an equivalent home would rent for and was fully aware that *owner's equivalent rent* was forecasting an ever-decreasing rate of return on home purchases. "You go through 50 or 60 years of experience with virtually no declines and you somehow believe that's the norm, and it is, except for the crisis that happens once in a century," Greenspan told me during our September 2008 interview.

A Warning Unheeded

One can forgive Greenspan for not foreseeing that a massive rise in mortgage defaults by people with poor credit who had been given mortgages they couldn't pay back would trigger an economic calamity. In 2002, while he may have seen a housing boom on the horizon, Greenspan was giving little thought to subprime lending's role in that boom. For Greenspan, subprime was still the small, niche market it had long been. And so, when one of his colleagues on the Federal Reserve's Board of Governors, Dr. Edward Gramlich, began warning of the dangers of subprime lending, it is somewhat understandable that Greenspan didn't pay him too much attention.

Dr. Edward (Ned) Gramlich died at the age of 68 on September 5, 2007, from acute myeloid leukemia. He served on the Fed's Board of Governors from 1997 until 2005 where he was the reigning expert on issues of community development and affordable housing. Gramlich strongly believed that the subprime mortgage market was a "valid innovation" that made homeownership a reality for 12 million households that might not otherwise have had access to credit. But Gramlich also saw the danger that was building in subprime. The effort to expand access to credit for those who had no credit history or those who had a poor one was becoming twisted into a vehicle for making loans to lots of unsophisticated borrowers who didn't have a realistic chance of paying the loans back, and Gramlich knew it.

He knew it because he had monitored the subprime market since its infancy and saw it changing. According to data from the Home Mortgage Disclosure Act, which Gramlich knew all too well, in 2005, roughly 20 percent of all subprime mortgages were made by banks and thrifts. Those institutions were heavily regulated, with federal supervisors visiting every three years to check the banks' routines for making loans and compliance with consumer protection statutes. Thirty percent of the subprime loans made in 2005 were extended by so-called "affiliates" of banks and thrifts. While these companies were not subject to routine visits by federal regulators, they were at least monitored and could be examined if problems were noted as a result of complaints or lawsuits. The rest of subprime loans were being made by companies like Quick Loan, Ameriquest, New Century, and

Countrywide Financial. They were supervised by the State of California, which meant they weren't supervised at all.

"I've been involved with literally hundreds of mortgage companies, and any of them that were licensed under the Department of Corporations [CA] have never been audited . . . not once," says Lou Pacific. "I've never heard of one audit. I've never heard of anyone I know of out here who was investigated, whether it was by local district attorneys or the FBI, at all, ever, in my thirty years in the business."

The Federal Reserve Board had the authority to change that state of affairs. It could apply rules to both banks *and* nonbanks such as the subprime lenders of Irvine, California. In 2002, Ned Gramlich tried to get the Fed to do just that by tightening lending standards across the board. Sheila Bair, who would eventually run the Federal Deposit Insurance Corporation (FDIC) during the worst banking crisis in 70 years, was a senior official at the Department of Treasury in 2002. From that post, she worked closely with Gramlich as the two tried in vain to impose some sort of standards on the Wild West of subprime lending.

Bair is one of those rare officials who give one confidence in government. She is an attentive, aggressive, straight-talking public servant with a razor-sharp mind—someone whose mouth is doing all it can to keep up with the complex thoughts that are coming from her brain. She first met Gramlich when he was a professor of economics at the University of Michigan and Bair was working for the New York Stock Exchange. The two had remained friends when Bair joined Gramlich in his pursuit of new, elevated lending standards.

Theirs was not an easy fight, in large part because of when they were waging it. In the early years of the housing boom, while there was some awareness of bad practices on the part of lenders, it was not costing anyone any money. As home prices rose ever more quickly, the people who had been on the receiving end of abusive mortgages were not getting abused. Remember the 2/28 mortgage? It hurt the borrower only when it adjusted, but if the equity in that borrower's home had risen in the intervening two years since he secured the mortgage, all he had to do was refinance. And as Lou Pacific said, he had customers who did just that year after year after year. "Who's complaining?" asked Bair rhetorically, when I interviewed her in the FDIC's offices. "Everybody's making money, you know, so what's the problem? I've been in Washington a long time and it's hard to get this town to move in a kind of preventative way. Right? There's got to be a big problem before you act."

Gramlich and Bair didn't have near enough political muscle to get the Fed to move. Their ragtag coalition of consumer groups and a handful of senators and congressmen was forced to settle for something far less than a law. "The avenues of doing something by regulation or statute didn't appear to be going anywhere," said Bair. She and Gramlich were left to hope that financial institutions would "volunteer" to apply tighter lending standards. "We tried to get some of the better players in the industry together to do best practices that we were hoping we could then get to be adopted more broadly. And then at least that would provide a benchmark and those who subscribe to the best practices would hopefully give consumers guidance about where they might be safer in doing business." Sheila Bair doesn't seem naïve—at least not anymore. The best practices effort she and Gramlich championed didn't stand a chance. The race to the bottom when it came to lending standards proved too strong even for the best of companies to avoid. After all, there was big money at stake.

Bair firmly believes that had she and Ned Gramlich gotten the regulations they wanted, rather than a bunch of voluntary guidelines, the financial crisis of 2007–2008 could have been avoided:

> I mean we're not talking about rocket science here. We're talking about underwriting at the fully indexed rate. Meaning when you make a loan, make sure they can take it when it resets, not just at the initial [teaser] rate. We're talking about verifying income. I mean, really, if there were two evils that drove this it was what we called teaser rate underwriting and not documenting income.

Bill Dallas agrees:

> Fully documenting the borrowers' income could have stopped it [the crisis]. If I had said to you, the borrower, "Fully document your income or you won't get this loan," it would have ended. But I'm one lender, right? So you know what happens to my volume if I do that and no one else does? It goes to zero.

One man could have imposed the lending standards that Gramlich sought. Standards that just might have averted the greatest financial crisis of our lifetime. But Alan Greenspan wasn't buying what Ned Gramlich was trying to sell. Greenspan recalls:

> "[Gramlich] came in and mentioned to me that there was a lot of these egregious practices going on and he said, you know, maybe we should try to do something." And I said "I'd be delighted, but I cannot see any way of succeeding," because unless we go in there with real law enforcement capability, which we did not have, [subprime lenders] would basically put in their windows "supervised by the Federal Reserve System" and they would have been far more egregious in their actions and basically done far more damage.

Greenspan believed that while the Fed could institute new lending standards, it did not have the resources or the power to actually enforce them. A new set of standards without effective enforcement would not, in Greenspan's opinion, have stopped New Century or First Franklin or Option One or Countrywide from their perilous race to be first with the worst. In fact, Greenspan submits that the addition of Federal Reserve oversight would have given these firms one more important piece of marketing power that would have helped them win even more customers.

There were also political considerations. "Had we tried to suppress the expansion of the subprime market, do you think that would have gone over very well with the Congress, when it looked as though we were dealing with a major increase in homeownership, which is of unquestioned value to this society—would we have been able to do that? I doubt it," posits the former Fed chairman.

Greenspan maintains that the laws needed to crack down on abusive lending practices were already on the books. If a borrower was lying about her income or a lender was submitting false information about that borrower's income, that constitutes fraud. The problem was not a lack of laws, says Greenspan, but a lack of enforcement:

> If there is egregious fraud, if there is egregious practice, one doesn't need new supervision and regulation, what one needs

is law enforcement. And to the extent that we were able to do that at the Federal Reserve, we made some progress. But the number of actual cases which we turned over to the Justice Department, which we unearthed in our examination processes was a very, very small number.

Sheila Bair remains unconvinced. "This market didn't have enough rules. It didn't. And when it did have rules, they weren't enforced vigorously enough." Bair believes that when the initial justification for subprime lending, namely that it was expanding homeownership, went away, the regulators should have moved in aggressively:

Seventy five percent of subprime loans ended up being for refinancings, and we saw many instances where mortgage originators would look for borrowers who had home equity and bad FICO scores and say "Let me give ya a cash-out refinancing . . . you want to pay off your bills, want a new pool, a new roof, whatever." And they'd call these things hybrid ARMS with a two-year fixed . . . and we've seen a lot of borrowers who were confused. They didn't understand they were going to have this big payment shock, or if they did they were just told, "Don't worry, you can just refinance that." These were not new homeowners, but people who had been in their homes for many years and might have had some equity before they got this product. It's a very sad chapter for the history of mortgage finance in this country.

Greenspan firmly believes his Fed did the right thing:

I know it goes against the grain of everybody who seems to think that you can push buttons here and there. It just doesn't work. You've got to recognize that these type of things are at the root, fraud, and we didn't have the proper structure, we didn't have the statutes that would enable us to go after it and in the end I'm not sure how well you could do. It's one thing to say "go regulate." But remember, the ultimate regulation is essentially a planned economy in which everything is constrained. You can't do anything without getting permission, and these systems collapse.

Greenspan, a true believer in the power of free markets if ever there was one, admits there are trade-offs to our freewheeling financial system. But given that that system has allowed us to attain standards of living few could ever have imagined when our founding fathers set the nation on its course, Greenspan believes the flaws in that system are worth living with. "There are many flaws in the system and the flaws in human nature are such that we cannot change them."

A Dream No More

Arturo Trevilla no longer lives in the dream house he bought in San Clemente, California, in May 2005. He, his wife and their three children now sleep in one room in a house they share with his wife's aunt, her husband, and their two children. The families also share the home with two other women.

When Trevilla signed up to get the financing to buy his former home, he didn't know that he was actually receiving two loans. One was a piggyback loan to finance his down payment on the $584,000 home and the other was the actual mortgage on the home. For two years, his payments were low and only four months after he bought the house its value had risen to $640,000. "The plans I had to start my own business, refinance the house after one year, were working perfectly." But then real estate prices stopped going up.

When Trevilla's mortgages adjusted higher in May 2007, the monthly payments exceeded $5,000. He struggled to stay current, charging most of his family's daily expenses to the credit cards he was offered after he bought the house. "I start using the credit cards, more and more and more and now I have a debt for credit cards, about $20,000."

When Trevilla lost his job, he was no longer able to keep up. His home was foreclosed on and promptly sold for $500,000. Trevilla was offered $3,000 if he moved out within two weeks:

> Because we need the money, we only took two weeks to move out. And it was just me and my wife and my three kids moving everything out. It was really difficult. And the really hardest part

of this thing was when I had to meet this guy from the bank to give back the keys to the house. I felt so bad. I was just with my oldest kid and right after I give the keys and get in the car, I start crying. Because I felt like part of our American dream was just on those keys.

Arturo Trevilla will probably file for bankruptcy. He is no longer planning to start an embroidery company, but working at whatever jobs come up whenever he can find work. His wife is cleaning homes. He sadly admits that his American dream of owning a home and a business may be gone forever.

Chapter 5

The Great Enabler

Mike Beuscher is the grim reaper of Orange County, California. He's a tall, pleasant-looking middle-aged fellow who makes his living clearing out homes after they have been foreclosed on, shattering the dreams of those who reached for a better life, even if they knew it couldn't last. For Mike Beuscher, business has never been better.

On the day we spent together, Beuscher gave me a tour of ground zero for the nation's housing bubble: Orange County, California. We saw $750,000 homes now covered in graffiti inside and out. We saw gardens, once filled with flowers, now dried up and empty. We saw cockroach infestations, garbage piled high, swimming pools half filled with strangely green water. We saw houses denuded of all their plumbing, all their wiring, and all their appliances. We saw rat-infested homes that must have slept 20 people. We saw the grimy, unsavory, sordid underbelly of the housing boom, where anyone could get a mortgage to buy virtually anything when they could afford nothing.

Mike Beuscher's license plate reads EVICTEM. It's nice to see a man who embraces his work. And when his black pickup pulls up in front of a house, the message is clear: It's time to go.

The homes that Mike Beuscher is sent to empty out and ready for sale are the homes in which people have stopped paying back their mortgages.

Mike Beuscher
Photo courtesy of CNBC.

Surveying the Wreckage of a Housing Bust with Mike Beuscher in Orange County, California
Photo courtesy of CNBC.

Mike Beuscher Shows Me a Future Breeding Ground for Mosquitoes
Photo courtesy of CNBC.

Mike Beuscher's License Plate
Photo courtesy of CNBC.

Once homeowners miss three monthly payments they are considered in default on their mortgage. Foreclosure used to come soon after. These days, however, given the torrent of mortgage defaults, foreclosure usually doesn't come for many months. But when it does, Mike Beuscher is there. Sometimes the people who live in these homes have been there for years, but more often than not, the homeowners Mike Beuscher is there to evict have barely been there long enough to memorize the address.

They seized a brief opportunity to own a piece of the American Dream and now they've been scattered, their empty and decaying homes left behind as a reminder of that dream gone bad.

These are the people who received mortgages from all those lenders who were happy to grant them without regard to income, debts, or ability to put money down.

Why would financial institutions extend mortgages to people who could not pay them back? That does not make sense.

If those financial institutions that lent the money actually had to be concerned about whether it would be repaid, they would no doubt have invested a bit more time and effort in making certain their borrowers had a good chance of doing just that. But subprime lenders such as New Century and Ameriquest and Quick Loan were not concerned about being paid back. They parted with that mortgage as soon as the ink on the application was dry, selling it a few moments after the buyer of the house received their money. And who was buying these pitiful mortgages from their originators? Who would want to own hundreds of billions of dollars' worth of mortgages reflective of a huge decline in lending standards when everyone one of them was at risk should housing prices even so much as level off?

Before we answer that question, we need to make a necessary detour back to that time and place when Americans who wanted a mortgage had to unburden themselves of every last bit of financial information they could spare in order to get one. The bank that gave them that mortgage would often keep the mortgage on its balance sheet as an asset. That's why lenders cared so much about whether they could repay that mortgage.

It wasn't the most efficient of financial dealings. The bank that granted your mortgage had only so much money to allocate to lending.

And while that amount might go up if its deposit base increased, the bank would never be in a position to give a mortgage to every potential homeowner who could afford one. It simply did not have enough money. That is why Fannie Mae was founded.

Fannie Mae and Freddie Mac Hit the Scene

In 1938, President Franklin D. Roosevelt and Congress created Fannie Mae (Federal National Mortgage Association) and gave it a mandate to buy mortgages from lenders, thereby freeing up capital for those lenders that they could use to extend more mortgages. Fannie Mae started as a rather modest effort. Its initial seed money of a billion dollars in capital was not going to let it buy up many mortgages. But because it was a government entity, it would in time be able to sell bonds to investors in order to raise more capital that it could then use to buy more mortgages. The bonds were an easy sell because people were sure they would be paid back since Fannie Mae was a government entity. Even after Fannie Mae went public in 1968, its status as a government-sponsored entity (GSE) allowed it to raise capital cheaply.

By 1982, Fannie Mae was funding one out of every seven mortgages made in the United States. And by then it had company. Freddie Mac (Federal Home Loan Mortgage Corporation) was launched in 1970, and, whereas its mission was identical to Fannie's, it operated its business a bit differently. Well into the 1980s, Fannie Mae retained most of the mortgages it bought. I know that first hand. In one of the lowest moments of my professional life, in October 1986 (I remember the date because the Mets were playing the Astros in the National League Championship Series), I spent three days at Fannie's northern Virginia headquarters pulling the mortgage-origination sheets of various borrowers (I was never told why). This, of course, was prior to the widespread use of computers and was one of a series of mind-numbing temporary jobs I held before thankfully embarking on a career in financial journalism.

Freddie Mac, unlike Fannie Mae, did not hold most of the mortgages it bought from lenders. It would bundle them together in what

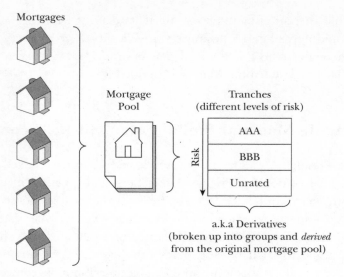

Figure 5.1   Residential Mortgage–Backed Securities

was initially called a *mortgage participation certificate* and eventually became known as a *mortgage-backed security* (MBS). The security, a pool of mortgages from across the country, paid its holders interest from the mortgage payments that were being made by homeowners (see Figure 5.1). It was normally rated triple-A (the highest credit rating) because American homeowners had a very good history of paying back their mortgages. Freddie Mac and eventually Fannie Mae (it offered its first mortgage-backed security in 1981 and would surpass Freddie in MBS issuance by 1992) would stand behind their mortgage-backed securities by agreeing to take back any mortgages in the pool that went bad. Of course, they received a nice fee for this *guarantor* service.

Fannie Mae and Freddie Mac would come to dominate the process for giving people mortgages in the United States even though neither company ever originated any of those mortgages. They did this by dictating to lenders the specific characteristics of the mortgages they would buy. If Fannie and Freddie told lenders they would only buy 30-year fixed-rate mortgages up to $250,000 with a loan-to-value of 80 percent from borrowers whose income had been well documented and who had FICO scores of over 700, then that is exactly what the majority of lending institutions in the United States would go out and originate. Fannie and Freddie set the standards under which they would purchase a mortgage and most financial institutions then conformed to those standards. That is how we got the term *conforming mortgage*.

Bill Dallas, who founded two mortgage lenders during his 30-year career in the mortgage business, watched Fannie and Freddie's rise to preeminence. "Lenders on their own are not strong enough to put mortgage-backed securities together and then issue them directly to investors," explains Dallas. "Most investors want a triple-A security and, long story short, the American business model for issuing mortgage-backed securities was Fannie and Freddie. Everyone knew they would stand behind the mortgages and their guidelines for underwriting mortgages had a history of working."

It wasn't the greatest business for the banks. There wasn't much money to be made in granting mortgages that would conform to Freddie and Fannie's standards, but for the decades of the eighties and nineties, that's just the way it was, a commodity business.

Yes, there were always exceptions. Mortgages above Fannie and Freddie's limit (which was $252,000 in 2002 and moved up to $333,000 by 2004) are known as *jumbo* mortgages and couldn't be sold to them, nor could the mortgages being originated by the first wave of subprime lenders in the early 1990s. But jumbo or subprime mortgages at that time were a tiny part of the business, which was centered for decades on originating mortgages that could be sold to Fannie and Freddie.

Fannie and Freddie Get a Timeout

Unlike the banks they were buying mortgages from, the mortgage business for Fannie and Freddie was a money train. As the amount of mortgages they bought reached into the trillions of dollars, the two public companies became among the most profitable corporations in the world. They were lauded by investors for their exceptional earnings growth and for the predictability of their performance. Investors flock to companies that show consistent patterns of growth in earnings, rather than volatility in earnings, which can send a stock price down one quarter and up the next. Maintaining that consistency in order to keep shareholders happy, while their businesses became ever more complex, was not an easy task. Eventually, in order to preserve that predictability, the companies would have to lie.

In November 2003, after an 11-month review of its accounting, Freddie Mac divulged that it had *understated* its earnings by $5 billion over the past three years. In an effort to make its business look predictable, Freddie's management had gone so far as to say it earned less money than it really did. The bulk of the accounting misstatement centered on Freddie's attempt to hedge its exposure to changes in interest rates by using derivatives. The admission by Freddie immediately turned regulators' attention to Fannie, and a similar accounting probe concluded 10 months later that it, too, had been guilty of manipulating its quarterly earnings so they would appear less volatile than they actually were. In Fannie's case, most of the shenanigans were to overstate profits, but the effect was the same. "Fannie Mae management intentionally smoothed out gyrations in its earnings to show investors it was a low risk company. It maintained a corporate culture that emphasized stable earnings at the expense of accurate financial disclosures," said a September 2004 report from Fannie and Freddie's chief regulator, the Office of Federal Housing Enterprise Oversight (OFHEO).

With their credibility in tatters, Congress up in arms, and their regulator, OFHEO, on the warpath, Fannie and Freddie retreated from the market they had dominated for the past 20 years. They began to buy fewer mortgages in a period where people were buying and refinancing more homes than ever before. "Knowing our industry, at its heart it's a people industry," explains Bill Dallas. "It's customer relationships at the front end and it's being driven by small and medium-sized mortgage bankers that deal with Fannie and Freddie on the back end. We were used to being led by two big actuaries, this oligopoly that owned the world. So we got all of our rules from those guys and that's what we did."

Suddenly, the leader of the U.S. mortgage market had gone home. And with no one to tell them what to do, the mortgage originators found themselves free to expand the guidelines they had lived with for years as long as they could find a buyer for the mortgages they were underwriting. That's when they met Wall Street. It was a union that would change the course of financial history.

Bill Dallas had dealt with Wall Street for much of his career. The lenders he had founded, First Franklin and Ownit, relied on Wall Street to buy their mortgages because most of them did not conform to Fannie and Freddie's guidelines. Dallas had been selling mortgages to Wall Street for quite some time, but now, with Fannie and Freddie on the sidelines, the floodgates had opened:

> The moment the mortgage originator met an unregulated Wall Street, those are two wires you don't want to cross. Because the mortgage broker is there to help the consumer get the house, buy the property. They're not naturally going to be saying "Oh, you know, I don't want to do this."

In 2003, roughly $4 trillion worth of mortgages were originated in the United States. It is the single largest amount of mortgages ever originated in U.S. history. In that same record year, 70 percent of those mortgages were sold to Fannie Mae and Freddie Mac. Seventy percent of that $4 trillion in mortgages conformed to Fannie and Freddie's guidelines.

In 2006, roughly $3 trillion worth of mortgages were originated in the United States. In that year, Fannie Mae and Freddie Mac accounted for only 30 percent of the secondary market. In three years, the share of mortgages they bought had gone from 70 percent of all the mortgages originated to 30 percent. The guidelines for lending that Fannie and Freddie had so diligently applied to the mortgage market were no longer operative. So who stepped in to fill the void and buy all those mortgages made during a period of declining lending standards? It was Wall Street.

Wall Street's investment banks had always played in the nation's mortgage market. It was Wall Street that funded the first subprime lenders by buying their mortgages and packaging them into mortgage-backed securities that were then sold to investors. Of course, those MBSs carried a much higher interest rate and a lower credit rating than anything sold by Fannie and Freddie because they carried a higher chance of default. Wall Street also bought the prime mortgages that were too big for Fannie and Freddie and also securitized and sold them. Wall Street played in the mortgage market, but had always played outside the conforming space that Freddie and Fannie dominated and it was always a relatively small space to play in.

Without Wall Street to buy their mortgages, firms like New Century, Ameriquest, and Quick Loan could never have existed. That's why they were known as *capital markets lenders*. They needed access to the capital markets, where bonds and stocks are sold, in order to have their mortgages packed into mortgage-backed securities and sold to investors. They got that access through Wall Street. But prior to 2004 their business, falling as it did in the "nonconforming" space, was still a small one.

Wall Street Takes Over

Myths have a way of being perpetuated long enough that they become unquestioned facts. One such myth that has been bruited about in 2008 and 2009 is that the lax lending standards of Fannie and Freddie promulgated the current crisis. It is *not true*. Wall Street rushed into the vacuum created by the *absence* of Fannie and Freddie in 2003–2005. It was Wall Street that took their market share and became the leader. It was Wall Street that encouraged mortgage originators of every kind to lower their standards by providing an endless supply of new capital to fund their mortgages. It was Wall Street that found willing buyers for U.S. mortgages around the globe in order to keep funding the mortgage market. It was Wall Street.

Michael Francis is one of those decent, hardworking guys who go to Wall Street, not because they think they're going to be a master of the universe, but because it's always proved a good place to support a family. Francis spent many of his 23 years in the mortgage business selling loans to Wall Street. Then he moved from the selling of mortgages to the buying of them, joining an investment bank in its capital markets division. Things went well for Francis. He would eventually run the capital markets side of the mortgage-origination business at a very well-known investment bank. He has asked me not to name it. While it is one of the best known of investment banks and it did participate fully in the mortgage business, it acted with a bit more sagacity than many of its competitors.

Michael Francis
Photo courtesy of CNBC.

Interview with Michael Francis
Photo courtesy of CNBC.

Francis explains his duties:

> I was in charge of our sales force. . . . It's really a buying force,
> but they're called salespeople. Their job was to go to smaller,
> mid-size as well as larger mortgage originators, banks as well as
> privately owned firms, and show them what programs we had,
> what our rates and what our prices were and get them to sell
> more loans to us.

Francis's job was to convince the people who ran mortgage-lending
operations that they would do well to sell their mortgages to his firm.
And how did he do that?

> The first part of our pitch is that we are Wall Street. We're the
> big bad guy that has all the access to capital that you need. That
> was the kind of lead-in, very typical of the way a lot of con-
> versations started with people. And then once we get past the
> handshakes and everything we really just try to do a good job of
> explaining what the differences are around our program versus
> our competitors'. We're going to give you a great price and a
> great rate and it's all going to be quick.

An investment bank's "mortgage program" comprises all the terms
under which that institution will buy mortgages from an originator. It
tells the originator what types of mortgages will be purchased and sets
the credit standards that must apply to those mortgages. It tells them
what the spread will be for those mortgages. A *spread* is the difference
between what it cost the lender to originate the mortgage and what
they are able to sell it for. Francis would also inform the lender of how
quickly they would be paid by the investment bank.

Quickness of payment was an important point for many mortgage
originators, who relied on a "warehouse" line of credit from a commercial or investment bank that gave them the short-term financing they
needed to fund the mortgages they were making. The average mortgage bank that Francis's firm dealt with had a net worth of between
three and five million dollars. It could borrow as much as 20 times that
net worth on its warehouse line of credit. "But if they're a mortgage

shop doing two or three hundred million a month, you can see they're going to produce more loans than they actually have capacity for. So the goal for them is to get the loan closed and have us, the end investor, buy that loan as quickly as possible to allow them to relieve the warehouse line so they had money in the tank to lend to the next guy," explains Francis.

If speed was of the essence, so was listening:

> The places that I worked did a pretty good job of reaching out to clients and asking for opinions on how we could shape our business to make it easier for them. Mortgage originators are on the ground beating the pavement, trying to get loans to make money. They are naturally gonna come up with a lot of different ideas on how they could generate more revenue through more loan volume. So we would reach out to those folks to help us try and twist and turn our programs to give them a program they could drive a ton more volume through.

Remember Bill Dallas's warning about "two wires you don't want to cross"? This is exactly what he was talking about. Michael Francis's firm and virtually every other Wall Street firm was not telling the originators what type of mortgage they would buy as Fannie and Freddie had always done. Instead, Wall Street firms were giving the originators free reign to tell them what mortgages they should be buying. And that's exactly what happened.

After Fannie and Freddie pulled back from the market, investors who bought mortgage-backed securities were left to look to Wall Street to quench their thirst for this fixed-income product. "It was an absolute shift," says Francis. "With so much liquidity moving away from Fannie Mae and Freddie Mac the world just completely shifted and there were more Wall Street private securitizations being done than Fannie Mae and Freddie Mac MBS." That shift gave Wall Street great power in dictating what mortgages would be originated and gave it pricing power versus Freddie and Fannie that it had never had. "We made it easier for a borrower to get a loan and then the cost of that loan on our side became much less. But for us, you wouldn't have to give as much documentation.

If the cost is the same, but you have to do less work, why wouldn't you go left versus going right?" explains Francis.

Wall Street's rising prominence was good news for Quick Loan Funding. "The way Wall Street works is if you have a need for a product, and you have a track record and you have volume showing that you can originate loans, then Wall Street will bend over backward to come out with a product to buy," says Lou Pacific, a 30-year veteran of the mortgage business who was a vice president at Quick Loan.

Just as Mike Francis said, the originators were going to Wall Street and asking them for the money to back a certain mortgage product. Lou Pacific recounts how the conversations would go:

> We'd approach Wall Street and say "Look, we have a product we think we can sell. And I can promise you $500 million a month or whatever in this product." And Wall Street would say, "Okay, this firm has a track record, they want this product, they're doing a lot of volume, let's give it to them." And let's say it was Merrill Lynch or Credit Suisse or whoever it was they went to, the word on the Street would spread that this product could be funded by Wall Street.

When the word got out, as it always did, that Merrill or another firm was funding a 95 percent loan-to-value mortgage for borrowers with a 580 FICO and above, the other subprime lenders would quickly try to horn in on the action. The result: A whole lot of mortgages would get signed up for people who fit the parameters of that particular program because the mortgage companies were being incentivized to sell that loan, knowing they had a willing buyer. "The incentive was that you would get a larger rebate on the loan. If a broker did a loan, the lender [Wall Street] would pay a certain amount of money for that loan," explains Pacific. "You would charge the borrower one or two percent of the loan as an origination fee and the lender would pay you up to three percent of the loan amount after the loan closed. It's called a rebate or yield spread premium and that's how you made your money." Pacific says the key to attracting Wall Street's largesse was having a track record, delivering volume, and putting people in mortgages at the highest rate possible.

Yes, that's right: The higher the rate on the mortgage, the more money the originator would be paid in that rebate by Wall Street. "If you could sell the loan for a higher rate and sell a lot of them at a higher rate, then Wall Street was in love with you. They would bend over backwards for you. They would buy anything you'd give 'em, just about," gushed Pacific. Subprime loans carried a low initial rate, but over the life of the loan a very high rate. It proved the perfect product for Wall Street. It also proved tempting for many of the subprime firms to convince consumers to take a subprime loan even if they qualified for a much lower-priced prime loan. "We used to get an awful lot of them [prime borrowers]," says Pacific unapologetically. "They were more concerned with the speed of getting a loan. And plus the average person doesn't understand where their credit ranking is, some don't think they can qualify for a good loan, but they can. So they'll call and if you sell a loan with a higher FICO score, you're going to make more money on it." Pacific claims that when he encountered such a person he would refuse his business and tell him to go to his local bank.

Pacific says that during his time at Quick Loan, he never saw Wall Street reject a mortgage booked by the firm. "Once you have volume, the word in this small community here in Irvine gets out. And Wall Street goes strictly by volume and how much money they can make off the loans. So if you have a company that's doing a lot of business at a high interest rate, which most of the subprime loans were, then they can make money on their end." There was one caveat: The person whose mortgage was sold to Wall Street had to make the first three monthly payments; otherwise the firm that bought the mortgage had the right to give it back to originators like Quick Loan. After three months, the originator was in the clear.

A Tsunami of Mortgages

At the investment bank where Michael Francis worked, business had never been better. The firm needed to buy $100 million worth of mortgages each month if it had any hope of breaking even, and when Francis was putting things together in 1997 and 1998 that was just a dream. By

2002, $100 million in mortgage volume became a reality, and that was before Fannie and Freddie's decision to retreat from the market.

"Within a six-month period of passing $100 million we were doin' $500 million and at this point we've gone beyond our wildest expectations," recalls Francis.

> And it's not just something that's putting out a little bit of money. It was putting out a fairly substantial amount of cash. And it was a dominant fixed income asset within the firm. If there were no mortgages, fixed income would be a blip on the radar of the earnings of the firm. Now mortgages were the reason fixed income became as big as it was.

The world was flush with cash and mortgage-backed securities were more popular than ever. China and other Asian countries were watching their economies soar and were wracking up huge surpluses of dollars in the process. Meanwhile, Russia and countries in the Middle East that relied on the export of oil to the United States were swimming in dollars they needed to invest. The result was unprecedented worldwide demand for dollar-denominated products like the American mortgage-backed security. And if a firm could provide that much-in-demand investment vehicle, it could try to cater to all the fixed-income needs of its clients. "Not only would we get them a mortgage bond. We had convertible bonds. We had corporate bonds. There was debt to be structured. Now we could capture every investor and bring them everything they could ever want. And why would they need to go across the street when they could get it all from us," explains Francis.

The bankers at Francis's firm had never been busier. They aggregated billions of dollars in mortgages that had been originated all over the United States, separated them into different buckets depending on the type of loan (fixed rate or adjustable), and went about creating the pools of collateral from which the mortgage-backed security bonds would spring forth. "We would start to evaluate what type of bonds were being produced by other Street firms and what type of bonds some of our clients were looking for and then create pools of collateral to meet their investment needs."

In fact, for many Wall Street firms it wasn't enough merely to be able to package mortgage-backed securities. They wanted in on the whole process, from origination to packaging to selling and even to the exacting business of collecting people's mortgage payments and distributing them to MBS holders (known as *servicing*).

Lehman Brothers was the first Wall Street firm to really embrace all aspects of the mortgage business. Bill Dallas remembers:

What was the Lehman model? "We wanna originate it. So we're gonna buy originators and we're gonna buy a servicer." And they were pretty successful at it. They bought BNC Mortgage. They bought Finance America. They bought their own servicer, called Aurora. Well, Wall Street firms are pretty much lemmings. If Lehman's doing it and they're successful at it, then Bear Stearns will go and Merrill will go and Goldman will go. They'll all go at it. And they all did.

And so they all were ready when Fannie and Freddie skipped off into their accounting scandal–induced timeout. The competition became fierce as Wall Street firms tried to land as many mortgages as they could lay their hands on, feverishly chasing the fees from creating the mortgage-backed securities that were now loved by investors around the globe. Lending standards quickly fell victim to the onslaught. Michael Francis remembers the slide in standards that led to the widespread use of mortgages that required no documentation of income.

"We started to loosen the guidelines," explains Francis, "at the same time that more and more people were wanting to get in on that loan. And was it the absolute best loan for every single borrower? I would say, generally speaking, no. But the path of least resistance is the biggest reason that loan became very popular." That and the knowledge that if one firm chose not to buy those mortgages, another surely would.

In 2003, Francis moved from one Wall Street firm to another. His new firm was a bit more cautious than the firm he had left and approached the stated income loans nervously. "We would have conversations about whether this was appropriate or not. For a very long time, everyone on our trading desk, and I think it's safe to say everyone, felt that on a stated income loan it was appropriate to make the borrower think twice about what they were putting on that application."

IRS form 4506 allows a mortgage lender to have access to a couple of key lines of a person's tax return in order to verify his or her income. Francis's firm tried to get lenders to have their clients sign that form. "We tried to implement it and we couldn't because it literally would have shut production down to zero, because none of our competitors, Wall Street, or not, were asking for that form." It's the same story as the one told by Bill Dallas. If the lender making the mortgage or the Wall Street firm buying it had demanded accountability, they would not have been better off as a result; they would have been out of the business.

Once Wall Street allowed mortgage lenders to not even try to keep their customers honest, there wasn't much left to do when it came to due diligence. There were automated tools that allowed the investment banks to ascertain whether the values ascribed to a particular property made sense given where the property was located. And the Wall Street firms could also verify that the borrower was a real person and the house they were buying or refinancing was in fact a house. But that's about it. Everything else was taken on faith. And most of that faith centered on housing prices. If the asset class kept appreciating, all would be well.

Business kept on building. In 2002, Michael Francis was ecstatic to see his firm pass the $100 million mark in the amount of mortgages it bought in a given month. By 2005, his firm was buying an average of $4 billion a month in mortgages. That's right: a 40-fold increase in monthly mortgage volume. And almost all of those mortgages were of the type sold by the guys in Irvine, California: They didn't come close to conforming to the long-held standards once enforced by Freddie Mac and Fannie Mae.

From Ownit to Out of It

The brief life of the mortgage lender Ownit, which was started by Bill Dallas in late 2003 and closed by him three years later, is instructive of the era. When Dallas founded Ownit, he wasn't looking to capitalize on the housing boom, but rather a coming housing *bust*. "The strategy was that the brutal facts are going to affect the industry, and we'll swoop in 'cause we have superior knowledge and better products. We were forecasting home price depreciation." But Dallas wasn't forecasting that Wall Street would take over the securitization market for mortgage-backed securities and in so doing extend the life of a small housing bubble while inflating it to enormous proportions.

Ownit's main focus was on giving mortgages to people who couldn't afford a down payment, but who had good credit. It offered 100 percent loan-to-value mortgages with an average size between $200,000 and $300,000 for borrowers who fully documented their income. Dallas says that space in the market, which he had originally pioneered when he ran First Franklin, had always seen low default rates.

Ownit started its life by buying a small mortgage company called Oakmont that had given out about $800 million worth of mortgages per year. "Less than a year later," recalls Dallas, "we were doing $4 billion and the second year we were doing more in a month than Oakmont did in the entire year of 2003. And that just shows you the insatiable appetite for what we were doing in the marketplace." Wall Street loved his product and Dallas was now focused on getting bigger.

But when you get that big, you have to find a stable source of those short-term loans called *warehouse* lines of credit that can fund your mortgages when you make them and before you sell them. Dallas turned to Merrill Lynch for a billion-dollar line of credit. He had dealt with the firm in the past when First Franklin sold it mortgages. Now, Merrill would get into business with Dallas's new firm, and to cement the relationship, Merrill Lynch bought a 20 percent ownership stake in the private company for $100 million in the fall of 2005. It wasn't long after that the wheels started to come off.

By 2006, with short-term interest rates hitting multiyear highs and the credit quality of available borrowers moving still lower, Ownit started to loosen its standards. It wanted to prove to Merrill that it had made a good decision in its choice of partner by showing it could grow. But to do so, Ownit started to do loans it had once avoided. "We never did a lot of it, but even doing a little bit was enough to taint the whole ship. When you mix no income verification with low FICO customers it's a bad mix," says a regretful Dallas. Making 100 percent loan-to-value adjustable-rate mortgages when interest rates are rising isn't the greatest place to be, and when you start to loosen your standards, things go downhill pretty fast. At least they did for Ownit.

> The business model—and by that I mean how much can you sell the loan for [to Wall Street] versus the risk that you're taking—was in question. And I can remember having a conversation with my board [of directors], saying, "Look we really have two questions that we have to answer. Do we want to continue to try and take that risk and continue to grow? Or do we wanna shrink?"

The decision was soon made for him. In September 2006, Merrill Lynch bought First Franklin, the first mortgage lender Dallas founded, from National City Bank for $1.3 billion. First Franklin wasn't seeing (or admitting) the problems that Ownit was, and Merrill was happy to focus its energy on its new acquisition rather than a firm that was still trying to play by the old rules of underwriting. "We shut it down in '06 because we could not navigate it any longer. And I just said, 'You know, I'm done. I've tried my best. It's gonna get worse. So we're out.' And what people don't understand is that one hundred percent loans should have gone to ninety-five percent, should have gone to ninety percent. We should had more down payment. We should had more income," laments Dallas.

In a normal mortgage world, the one ruled by Freddie and Fannie for all those years, when interest rates started going up, mortgage volume should have started going down. And for prime borrowers, that's just what happened. The issuance of prime mortgages fell sharply in late 2004 and stayed down as the Federal Reserve raised interest rates from the historic low of 1 percent in June 2004 to a high of 5.25 percent two years later. But instead of overall mortgage issuance falling, the drop in prime mortgages was replaced by an avalanche of subprime and alt-A mortgages.

Bill Dallas had been around long enough to know something was amiss. He had never seen a market where volume went up while interest rates did as well. The proliferation of toxic mortgage products and the willingness of Wall Street to buy them created demand that should not have been there and wasn't during any previous interest rate cycle. Bill Dallas shut down rather than make mortgages that were going to go bad only months after they had been funded.

Back from the Grave

If only our story ended there. But like a horror movie in which a character has avoided a bloody death until foolishly venturing back to the place where the murder was committed, so too did Fannie and Freddie decide it was time to return to the scene of the crime. Their timeout was over and now their managements eyed a market that was no longer built for their rules. As subprime and alt-A loans ballooned to a bigger and bigger percentage of the mortgage market, the risk-management restrictions Fannie and Freddie had in place limited each company's involvement with those type of mortgages. They might want to once again dominate the mortgage-backed security market, but they were not going to be able to do that unless they could buy most of the mortgages that were being made.

In June 2005, Fannie Mae found itself at a "strategic crossroads," according to a then-confidential presentation prepared for Fannie's then-CEO, Daniel Mudd. The document, unearthed by Representative Henry Waxman's Committee on Oversight and Government Reform, lays out two clear choices. Fannie Mae could either "stay the course" or "meet the market where the market is."

Staying the course meant sticking with the prime, well-documented mortgages that had always been Fannie and Freddie's bread and butter. But the real "revenue opportunity," according to the confidential presentation, was in buying subprime and other alternative mortgages. The presentation acknowledged that investing in the riskier mortgages would bring higher credit losses and exposure to unknown risks. But it would also mean bigger profit margins and it would satisfy their overseers in Congress, who were urging the GSEs to make credit more widely available to borrowers who had not always been its recipients.

Fannie and Freddie were getting bullied by the lenders of Irvine, California, who taunted the two companies with their newfound access to Wall Street's securitization pipeline. "You need us more than we need you," was the subprime lenders' new mantra and Fannie and Freddie took the bait. After all, while they were government-sponsored entities, they were also public companies with a responsibility to drive profits for their shareholders, profits that would also reward their management.

In 2004, Freddie Mac's chief risk officer sent an e-mail to CEO Richard Syron urging the company to stop purchasing loans that had no income or asset requirements as soon as "practicable." Freddie had only recently begun some small purchases of these loans, which the chief risk officer warned were targeted to borrowers who would have trouble qualifying for a mortgage if their financial position were adequately disclosed. Syron fired him.

Suffice it to say, as the materials furnished by Waxman's committee indicate, Fannie and Freddie plunged deep into the parts of the mortgage market they had once avoided. They were also cheered on for doing so by influential congresspersons such as Democratic Representative Barney Frank from Massachusetts. The decision cost them both dearly. Had Fannie and Freddie stayed on the sidelines, they would have had more than a fighting chance to survive the housing market's implosion instead of being consumed by it.

With Fannie and Freddie back in the game and competing vigorously with Wall Street to buy subprime and alternative mortgages, the pace of securitization hit previously unimagined heights, which meant the amount of money available to these subprime borrowers skyrocketed as well. In 2005, 80 percent of subprime mortgages were being securitized and sold to voracious investors around the world. The subprime mortgage had become a chief export of our country.

Alan Greenspan believes the roots of the credit crisis spring directly from this fact. "Were it not for the securitization and essentially spreading those mortgage-backeds across the world, the subprime problem would have been constrained to the United States. 'Cause I know of no single mortgage that is subprime which is held outside the United States other than in securitized form," says the former Fed chairman.

The tremendous demand for mortgage-backed securities made up of subprime mortgages had begun at the early part of the housing boom in 2003 and 2004, when rising home prices enabled subprime borrowers to refinance their way out of any financial trouble. The rate of return on mortgage-backed securities from those years was high because people kept paying their mortgages or even repaid them in full due to sales or refinancings.

Greenspan says their mistake was assuming the future would be like the past. "The basic problem that they created was they perceived delinquencies and defaults were very small, as they were in the early stages of the subprime market, because home prices were rising."

No one ever seemed to ask what would happen if housing prices started to fall.

Chapter 6

Complicity

There would have been no credit crisis and therefore no economic crisis if not for the complicity of the rating agencies. They were the oil that greased all the moving parts in the great machine Wall Street constructed to package up and sell U.S. subprime mortgages around the world. Their job was to protect investors from that machine. Instead they protected the profits they were making from it.

In our financial system, three companies known as *rating agencies* dominate the business of deciding how safe or unsafe a particular piece of debt is. Those companies are Moody's Investors Service, Standard & Poor's, and to a lesser extent, Fitch Ratings. Standard & Poor's (S&P) is owned by the McGraw-Hill Company. Fitch is owned by France's Fimilac. Moody's is the only public company of the three and boasts the added credibility of having Warren Buffett among its largest investors.

Moody's went public in September 2000, when it was spun off from its longtime parent Dun & Bradstreet at the behest of that company's shareholders, who believed the separation would lead to better days for both. The company was founded in 1909 by John Moody when he published a manual entitled *Analysis of Railroad Instruments*, which introduced a system of opinions about the creditworthiness of

Table 6.1   Moody's Long-Term Rating Definitions

Aaa	Obligations rated Aaa are judged to be of the highest quality, with minimal credit risk.
Aa	Obligations rated Aa are judged to be of high quality and are subject to very low credit risk.
A	Obligations rated A are considered upper-medium grade and are subject to low credit risk.
Baa	Obligations rated Baa are subject to moderate credit risk. They are considered medium-grade and as such may possess certain speculative characteristics.
Ba	Obligations rated Ba are judged to have speculative elements and are subject to substantial credit risk.
B	Obligations rated B are considered speculative and are subject to high credit risk.
Caa	Obligations rated Caa are judged to be of poor standing and are subject to very high credit risk.
Ca	Obligations rated Ca are highly speculative and are likely in, or very near, default, with some prospect of recovery of principal and interest.
C	Obligations rated C are the lowest-rated class of bonds and are typically in default, with little prospect for recovery of principal or interest.

NOTE: Moody's appends numerical modifiers 1, 2, and 3 to each generic rating classification from Aa through Caa. The modifier 1 indicates that the obligation ranks in the higher end of its generic rating category; the modifier 2 indicates a midrange ranking; and the modifier 3 indicates a ranking in the lower end of that generic rating category.

railroad bonds. The business of judging creditworthiness evolved from there. By 1914, Moody's Investors Service was incorporated with the goal of providing a rating on virtually any bond, whether corporate or government, that was issued at the time. The rating would tell prospective borrowers how likely they were to be repaid in a timely manner. A high rating (Aaa) meant a very high likelihood of repayment and hence little risk, whereas a lower rating (B) meant the opposite. Table 6.1 shows the rating system used by Moody's.

The rating agencies are not regulators. And yet, for a long time they were treated like regulators. That's because as their business developed, their ratings became the key benchmark used by many investors to buy bonds. Insurance companies, pension funds, money market funds, and endowments would be forbidden by their charters from buying debt that was not *investment grade*. And who decided what was and was not investment grade? The rating agencies.

In fact, some state insurance regulators mandate that companies they oversee may buy only securities that receive the top four ratings from *nationally recognized statistical rating agencies* (NSROs), which means Moody's, S&P, and Fitch. Whether by law or not, the fact that so many big institutional investors rely on the rating agencies to tell them what they can and cannot buy has given those agencies enormous power.

The rating agencies' power has been magnified by investors, who demand that corporations maintain certain levels of investment-grade ratings on their debt or face arduous consequences. A ratings downgrade from S&P or Moody's can force a company to post more collateral. It's what's known as a *ratings trigger*. When AIG was selling credit insurance on mortgage-backed securities, it held very little in reserve to pay those claims should it be forced to do so because it had an excellent credit rating. But when its credit rating was downgraded by S&P and Moody's, AIG was forced to increase its reserves on all sorts of transactions because its ability to pay was no longer a lock. AIG couldn't come up with the billions in collateral it needed and turned to the government for a bailout.

A credit rating downgrade can also result in a company having to pay more to borrow. That's why corporations fight to stay in the good graces of the rating agencies. The better or higher the credit rating, the cheaper it typically is for a corporation to borrow money. The lower the rating, the more it will cost that company to borrow money.

And if all that isn't enough, the rating agencies have one more advantage that gives their ratings additional power. In their evaluation of credit, the agencies are allowed to receive confidential information from the creditors to aid their decision. A credit rating, therefore, is no ordinary opinion, but one based on information that other market participants do not have.

With all of that power at their disposal, through the years, the rating agencies expanded their aegis to include not only corporate bonds, but commercial paper, preferred stock, syndicated bank loans, municipal bonds, infrastructure projects, bank deposits, and mutual funds. If there was anything sold to investors that required a judgment on whether the borrower would pay the money back, the rating agencies were there to tell you the answer.

Not that their answers were always correct—far from it. Because they have always looked at history to determine the creditworthiness of a borrower, the rating agencies have often been accused of acting too late to issue downgrades to do investors any good. It really doesn't help an investor who owns a bond of a company after bad news is out. Still, even if they didn't do a great job of weeding out the good credits from the bad, the agencies avoided much scrutiny. They had a solidly profitable business that did better when the issuance of bonds was high and less well when the bond market was quiet. But with the growth of *structured products*, the credit agencies' business began to boom.

When we think about publicly traded debt, we tend to think of bonds issued by corporations or the government. But debt, more broadly speaking, can take many forms, all of which have the common purpose of funding some kind of investment. A mortgage-backed security, for example, is not really a bond, but a structure created at one moment in time to fund the purchase of mortgages. And unlike a bond sold by a corporation, which generally has the same characteristics as every other bond being sold at that time and reflects the credit quality of the issuer, a mortgage-backed security can be carved up into different levels of risk. That is called *structuring*.

The structuring process finds its roots in the beginnings of mortgage securitization more than 30 years ago. A man named Lou Ranieri is credited with being the inventor of securitization in the private sector. In 1977, while at Bank of America, he put together a pool of mortgage loans and sold a debt security against the loans. As cash flowed in from the mortgages, debt holders got paid. But Ranieri had a problem. He couldn't sell his newfangled security to the biggest pools of capital out there, pension funds and mutual funds, because it wasn't eligible to be rated by a rating agency. No rating, no big buyers. So Ranieri spent a year lobbying Congress to get these securities eligible under the Employer Retirement Income Security Act (ERISA) and, once he succeeded, the rating agencies stepped in with ratings. A market was born.

Ranieri's early mortgage securitizations were known as *pass-throughs*, ancestors to the highly complex structures that would constitute mortgage securitizations in the future. Dr. Joseph Mason, professor of finance at Drexel University, Senior Fellow at the Wharton School of business, and an expert on securitization, says the problem with those early pass-through structures was that by throwing all those mortgages together and selling only one piece of debt based on them, the rating given that debt was not going to be the best one available.

If I can sell the highest-rated debt (AAA at S&P or Aaa at Moody's), I can sell it at the lowest interest rate. If I put together a pool of mortgages that pays me an average of 7 percent interest and can fund most of it by selling securities that are triple-A rated and therefore pay only 5 percent interest, I can make some good money on that interest rate spread. That's why the goal of an issuer is to obtain the highest credit rating for the debt it is selling. That desire is what leads to structuring.

The typical mortgage-backed security might consist of as few as 1,000 loans or as many as 25,000. The rating agencies' job is to determine the expected loss for the entire pool of mortgages and determine the amount of triple-A bonds, AA bonds, and so on that can be issued against that pool.

"It's just like the old economics 101 example of having different movie theater prices for matinees and for evening tickets," says Professor Mason.

> We want to carve up the market into as many segments as we can. So if we can issue some triple-A-rated debt and sell that to investors who desire a safe investment, on the other end of the scale we're left with some very risky debt that some investors like and are willing to buy. And that is the structuring process: how much risky and how much riskless debt to sell to fund that pool of mortgages.

Moody's the Money Maker

Moody's couldn't have chosen a better time to become a public company. Wall Street was about to embark on its fee-induced rampage into the mortgage-backed securities market, and who better to take along for the ride than the rating agencies? At Moody's, profits would quadruple between 2000 and 2007 and it would boast the highest profit margin of any company in the S&P 500 for five of those years. Moody's operating margins during these years hovered slightly above 50 percent. Is it any wonder that Warren Buffett liked its business? It wasn't rating corporate bonds that gave rise to this bounty; it was the incredible growth of Moody's *structured products* business.

Sylvain Raynes and Ann Rutledge, who are husband and wife, joined the structured finance group of Moody's in 1995. They each spent five years at Moody's before leaving to start a consulting firm in structured finance. Long before it became popular, the two were voices in the wilderness, warning of the reckless path being trod by the rating agency they once worked for when it came to its ratings of structured investment products.

Rutledge began her career with Moody's in Hong Kong. It was the dawn of the age of structured finance, but even then, Moody's could smell profits. Rutledge says it wasn't hard to figure out why. "There was a consulting element to the business that allowed us to grow the business in a way that wasn't possible with corporate ratings." Consultants typically get hired by a company for months or years. It was the same with structured finance. Moody's or S&P would be called on again and again to advise the banks that were creating structured products how to do so to get the best rating.

In the corporate debt world, in which the rating agencies had long held sway, there wasn't much room for improvising. Sylvain Raynes explains:

> In corporate finance, the corporation preexists the rating. When you start working for Moody's, IBM has existed for over fifty years, Coca-Cola has existed for at least a hundred years. It's very difficult for you to come in and say, "You know what, you guys have all been wrong for a hundred years."

But in structured finance there is no history. When you take pools of assets and repackage them into a structure, it's not an operating company, it is simply a portfolio. "The ratings and the corporation are born at the same time," says Raynes, "so, if you say, 'this is triple-A,' who's to say that you are incorrect? There was no benchmark. There was nothing beforehand to tell you that there was anything that wasn't triple-A. You are creating your own reality."

That reality became a huge profit center for the rating agencies as the wave of residential mortgage-backed securitizations washed over them.

That's because the rating agencies get paid by the issuer to rate their products. That's right: The investment banks that were slobbering all over themselves trying to buy mortgages from firms like Quick Loan Funding so they could pool them together into a residential mortgage-backed security (RMBS) were the same investment banks paying Moody's or S&P or Fitch to assign a rating to their handiwork. It's as though the home team in a baseball game was paying the umpire's salary. And if you're wondering how that payment system doesn't prejudice the process of awarding a rating, you're not alone.

It wasn't always this way. Until the early 1970s, the rating agencies relied on investors to furnish the bulk of their revenues. They derived their income from publishing rating manuals and offering investment advisory services. But once Lou Ranieri came along with his mortgage-backed securities, a structure that didn't exist until it was created by Ranieri and anointed with a rating, the agencies realized there was more money to be made with the *issuer-pays* model. Rating so-called "structured products" remained a small business for many years; little attention was paid to the potential conflict of interest raised by the issuer-pays model.

Thirty years later, with structured products contributing the bulk of profitability for the rating agencies, payment by the issuer had become standard practice. The rating agencies maintain that the issuer-pays model benefits the market because once a rating decision is made, it is widely and publicly disseminated, aiding transparency. In testimony given before the House Committee on Oversight and Government Reform in September 2008, the men who run the three major rating agencies all made the same point: Potential conflicts exist regardless of who pays for ratings, and the issuer-pays model works well as long as the agencies *manage the potential conflict of interest* inherent in that model. They, of course, say that's exactly what they do. Others disagree.

All I can say is that, other than the guys who run these firms, very few people seem to think they were focused on awarding the most accurate rating rather than doing the most deals. Awarding a rating to one structured transaction could bring in as much as half a million dollars in fees, compared to about $50,000 for the average bond issue. With that kind of money at stake, is it any wonder that Moody's, a newly public company, would think twice before disappointing an investment bank by not awarding one of its deals the desired credit rating?

The men who run the agencies claim their ratings are nothing more than an opinion. They say that in giving those opinions all the agencies are doing is exercising their First Amendment rights. "Because the future cannot be known, credit analysis necessarily resides in the realm of opinion," testified Moody's CEO, Raymond McDaniel, when he appeared before the House Committee on Oversight and Government Reform. "Rather than being simple default/won't default statements, our ratings are opinions about the risk of outcomes in the future with degrees of uncertainty."

Even if that is true, the people who rendered those opinions at Moody's or S&P tell me they believed in their role as policeman for the capital markets. "The role of ratings agencies and the people working in them," says Raynes, "was simply to provide an honest, or more honest opinion than the banker who wants the deal to happen. And to provide some sense of integrity to the process." Raynes and Rutledge believe that integrity was lost the day Moody's went public. "It used to be Moody's Investors Service; then it became Moody's Issuers Service," says Raynes. "When they switched their allegiance from the investors to the issuers, from trying to do the right thing to trying to make deals happen, they became part of the problem, as opposed to part of the solution."

Repeat Customers

Jerome Fons worked for Moody's for 17 years until August 2007, and held a variety of senior positions at the company. In testimony before Congress, Fons said that following Moody's spinoff from Dun & Bradstreet, management's focus increasingly turned to maximizing revenues.

> Stock options and other incentives raised the possibility of large payoffs. Managers who were considered good businessmen and women—not necessarily the best analysts—rose through the ranks. Ultimately this focus on the bottom line contributed to an atmosphere in which "rating shopping" could flourish.

Rating shopping, as its name implies, is the shopping by investment banks for the ratings they desire for their structured transaction. If they don't get satisfaction with one rating agency, the investment banks hold out the threat of simply taking their business and their fee elsewhere. "It was relatively easy for the major banks to play the agencies off one another because of the opacity of the structured transactions and the high potential fees earned by the winning agency," testified Fons. And because the investment banks are coming back time and again to get ratings on new deals, there is always the implicit threat that if they are not pleased with a credit rating on one transaction, they may not come back to the same rating agency to get its opinion on the next transaction.

Professor Joseph Mason uses the analogy of a car salesman:

> If I just sell you my car one time and you drive away in the car and it breaks down up the street, too bad. But if I'm selling you a car week after week or month after month and you're a repeat customer and you drive away and the engine falls out up the block, I'm gonna take care of you. Because I'd like to see you come back. So there's this fundamental feature of repeated games. Somebody repeatedly bringing deals to the rating agencies. You're gonna take care of them. Make sure that you don't come down too hard on their ratings.

And then there was dinner. Michael Francis says many firms wined and dined the rating agency analysts in hopes of getting lower costs of credit:

> A topic of conversation on our trading desk regularly was why we weren't getting the same levels of enhancement at the same cost structure as some other firms. And one could only speculate that it was because we didn't have the relationship with them. We didn't take those folks out to dinners and lunches and so forth.

It could not have been easy for analysts to stand their ground. Raynes says a lack of training coupled with relentless pressure from the investment banks and the firm's own management made it awfully tough to not come up with the desired rating.

Most people at rating agencies are honest individuals. They're trying to feed their family. There's no evil intent. It's simply that they're overwhelmed. They don't have the tools. They don't have the training. They were thrown to the wolves. Someone [the banker] who makes a million dollars a year is calling you and you make a hundred thousand maybe, who's going to win? Eventually you're ground down. If you don't have the support from the management, from your boss and his boss, then you are going to have to give up.

A consulting type of relationship is born. The investment bank structures a mortgage-backed security deal looking for a certain percentage of it to be rated triple-A and the credit rating agency tells it what it needs to do in order to make that a reality. "It becomes a discussion between you and the financial arranger," says Rutledge. Since there has never been a rating on this particular pool of mortgages, the analyst has free reign.

In their testimony before Congress, the executives who run Moody's, S&P, and Fitch all said their firms simply rate these deals and are not involved in any way in structuring them. But Joe Mason and Sylvain Raynes, among many others, take issue with that belief. It was only the rating agency that could define what triple-A meant for any deal and therefore dictate what the structure should look like. When Ann Rutledge talks about the consulting element of the business, that's what she means. "For a rating agency to say 'I did not structure these securities' is like a woman saying, 'I did not structure my baby.' It's just not credible," says Raynes. "The rating agency tells you where the boundary is on a deal. It's the arbiter that says this deal can have ninety-seven percent triple-A issuance, but not ninety-eight percent," explains Mason. "The investment bank just does what an investment bank does. It takes the securities to market."

Even if we assume the rating agencies' analysts were overmatched and their managements more interested in deal volume than accuracy, there was still a chance these firms could have stood their ground. After all, they had been rating these mortgage-backed securities for over 30 years. Surely, they had models that gave them strong predictive abilities when it came to forecasting mortgage defaults. In fact, some of their managers testified to just such a strength in front of Congress.

Vickie Tillman, an executive vice president at S&P, told the Senate's Banking, Housing and Urban Affairs Committee that, "S&P has been rating RMBS for thirty years and has developed industry-leading processes and models for evaluating the creditworthiness of these transactions. As a result, S&P has an excellent track record of assessing RMBS credit quality."

What Vickie Tillman didn't say during her testimony on September 27, 2008, was that S&P, like Moody's and Fitch, had nowhere near that amount of experience with the exotic mortgage products being offered by all those lenders in Irvine, California. Yes, S&P had been giving ratings to mortgage-backed securities for a long time. But those were yesterday's mortgages—30-year fixed-rate mortgages to people with good credit ratings. S&P had no clue how a stated income, 95 percent loan-to-value mortgage given to a person with poor credit was going to perform over time, because those kinds of mortgages didn't exist in any real way until 2003.

Joseph Mason testified in front of the same Senate Committee on the day Tillman delivered her remarks. He says many of the other panelists bristled when they heard her laud S&P's 30 years of experience. "We all thought to ourselves, 'wait a minute,'" says Mason.

> The pay-option adjustable rate mortgage for a subprime borrower has been around since 2005. You have nowhere near thirty years' exposure to that product and experience with that product. How can you possibly rate it? Similarly, a lot of the deeper subprime loans have been around for three to five years at most and have not been tested through the cycle. It's very difficult to build a model when you don't have that type of experience with the product.

It's also hard to build a model that will work when you don't want to spend the money to do it. That's apparently what happened at S&P, according to the man who for 10 years (1995–2005) ran the division that rated RMBS. Frank Raiter (yes, that's really his name) told

Congress that S&P had worked hard to build a sophisticated, statistically based model that estimated the default rate and loss severities of individual loans and pools of mortgages. The key to increasing the accuracy of that model was to keep feeding it the data from new mortgages. The more mortgages the model could process, and the longer the historical performance of those mortgages it could judge, the more accurate its future readings would be. And that's just what S&P was doing until 2001, when a new version of the model was developed that used the pertinent information on how 2.5 million mortgages were performing.

Acquiring data, performing the statistical analysis of that data, and using the technology necessary to incorporate what the model was telling S&P into its ratings process was expensive. It required lots of people to do it, but Raiter says that by 2001, "the focus at S&P was profits for the parent company, McGraw-Hill; it was not on incurring additional expense." The company's analysts were busy making money from rating structured transactions, and the allocation of resources to a part of the business that didn't produce profits was frowned on. The new model was never implemented.

Had it been, S&P could have been drawing analysis from the data on 9.5 million mortgages by 2004, including quite a few of the new types (subprime, option ARM, alt-A) that had recently hit the market. Raiter believes S&P would have foreseen a sharp rise in delinquencies in those new non-prime products and subsequently increased its loss estimates on the pools of mortgages it was rating. Higher loss estimates would have led to lower credit ratings, which would have made the transactions more expensive for the bank that was creating the product. Make it expensive enough and there's a good chance the banks would stop doing it altogether.

Finally, there was fraud. A factory worker like Arturo Trevilla inflated his income more than fourfold, and the mortgage broker who gave him his loan was happy to oblige. So was the investment bank that bought that loan and stuck it in a mortgage-backed security. But what about the rating agency? Shouldn't it be on the lookout for fraudulent mortgages like the one given Arturo Trevilla? The answer is a resounding *no*.

Ann Rutledge learned that early on in her tenure at Moody's. She uncovered what she thought was fraud in a particular deal and brought it to the attention of the managing director who was her boss. "I asked her, 'I think there might be some fraud in this deal—what should I do?' And she said, 'Moody's doesn't look at fraud. We're not responsible for fraud.' I said, 'So what do I do?' and she said, 'Do the best you can.'"

Rating agencies do not verify the accuracy of the information contained on the mortgage application. They rely on a guarantee from the issuer of the mortgage-backed security that the information is correct. But we already know from Michael Francis that the extent of due diligence conducted by the investment bank stopped at making sure the house was a house and the person who was borrowing was a person. All those mortgages given to people who had stated their income and lied about it were never being checked. Nothing of true relevance to the creditworthiness of the customer was being verified—not by the originator of the mortgage, not by the investment bank that created the RMBS, and not by the firm whose opinion brought that security to life with a credit rating that would guarantee its ability to be sold.

In 2006, Moody's reported net income of $750 million, most of it derived from its structured finance business. In the company's annual report on the year, CEO Raymond McDaniel gushed, "I firmly believe that Moody's business stands on the 'right side of history' in terms of the alignment of our role and function with advancements in global capital markets."

He should have known, because by 2006 the mortgage market had advanced far beyond the simple residential mortgage-backed security to a structured product with fewer initials, but a much bigger bite: the *collateralized debt obligation* (CDO).

Chapter 7

The Securitization
from Hell

Alan Greenspan: I've got some fairly heavy background in mathematics.

David Faber: I would think you're one of the few people who might understand what a CDO really is.

Greenspan: But some of the complexities of some of the [financial] instruments that were going into CDOs bewilders me. I didn't understand what they were doing or how they actually got the types of returns out of the mezzanines and the various tranches of the CDOs that they did. And I figured if I didn't understand it and I had access to a couple hundred PhDs, how the rest of the world is going to understand it sort of bewildered me. But here I am observing all of these very sophisticated investors trying to buy more of this stuff than existed.

Faber: Yes, but this goes to my original point in my question to you. If Alan Greenspan can't understand how they are getting to where they are getting on these particular structured products, then how are any of these investors supposed to understand?

Greenspan: Well, we learned the answer to that. They didn't.

—Transcript from an interview with
Alan Greenspan, September 4, 2008

T he *collateralized debt obligation* (CDO) may well go down in history as the worst thing anyone on Wall Street has ever thought up. But like so many other financial products invented by people who really liked math in school, the CDO was a harmless three-lettered security when it made its debut in 1987. That being said, it does seem fitting that the CDO was invented at the investment bank of Drexel Burnham Lambert. Drexel, home of junk (high-yield) bond kingpin Michael Milken, would famously fail in 1990 after Milken's indictment and the collapse of the junk bond market he had created. But the CDO lived on.

While it may be quite difficult to understand why anyone ever bought a CDO (as Greenspan makes clear), it isn't that difficult to understand how they were created and structured.

The Making of a CDO

CDOs (at least the ones we are dealing with) were created from mortgage-backed securities and structured in the same way as mortgage-backed securities.

A mortgage-backed security is created when thousands of home loans are purchased and pooled together by an investment bank that finances that purchase by issuing mortgage-backed securities to investors. The investors are paid interest from the mortgage payments coming into the pool. The pool usually includes different classes of securities (called *tranches*) that carry a sliding scale of interest rate based on their risk (see Figure 7.1). The lowest interest rate would be paid to those investors who bought the tranche with the least risk (AAA).

If a mortgage-backed pool issued eight separate tranches of securities, the AAA tranche would be the first to receive its payments from the mortgage pool, and so on down to the final tranche, which carries a higher interest rate because it carries more risk. If the pool starts to have less money coming in because some people stop paying their mortgages, those losses are taken first by the lowest tranche until it is wiped out and then move up through the capital structure.

Investment banks aim to have the AAA-rated tranche of securities be the largest because it pays the lowest interest rate. If a bank has

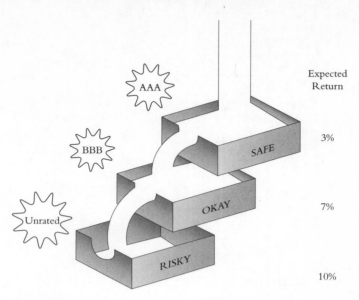

Figure 7.1   Different Classes of Securities, or Tranches

assembled a group of subprime mortgages that pay an average interest rate of 7 percent and manages to have most of the securities issued
be rated AAA, it won't have to pay those investors anywhere near that
interest rate. The less it needs to pay, the more it can keep in so-called
spread. The lower-rated tranches will bear a higher interest rate. But at
the end of the day, the investment bank is trying to make sure that
while everyone gets paid the interest they are owed, more money comes
into the pool than has to go out to pay that interest. That money, along
with its fee for arranging the deal, is how the bank gets paid.

An easy way to imagine all of this is to think of the pool of mortgages filling up with principal-and-interest payments that cascade down
into a series of smaller pools. Consider it a small waterfall. When the first
pool is filled up with payments, all the pools into which it feeds will also
be filled. And if times are good, after the final pool is filled, there may
still be some money left over for the bank that put it all together. But if
people stop paying their interest and principal and the first pool doesn't
completely fill, the cascade may not make it all the way to the final pool.

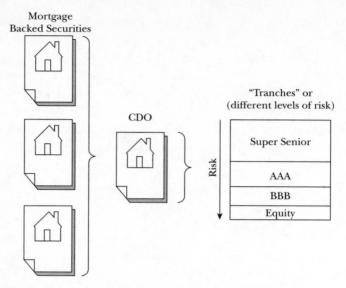

Figure 7.2   The Structuring of Collateralized Debt Obligations

If the payments really dry up, many of the pools into which the first pool feeds may not have any money flowing into them.

A CDO is structured in the same fashion as a mortgage-backed security. It is sliced up into different sections that have varying degrees of risk and payment. But instead of being comprised of thousands of mortgages, a CDO is comprised of hundreds of mortgage-backed securities (Figure 7.2).

The math behind a CDO, however, remains the same. When the securities owned by the CDO get their payments, the money is pooled yet again and sent out to the investors who have bought an interest in that CDO. It's just that simple, but the rest of the story isn't.

Tough to Kill

The CDO was born out of necessity. Wall Street needed to find a way to meet investor demand for a particular asset, even when there weren't enough of those assets in existence to actually meet the demand.

Back in 1987, the firm of Drexel Burnham Lambert had created an enormous market for borrowers who had previously been all but cut off from the chance to raise money through the sale of debt. These borrowers were not investment grade, but junk. Thanks to the efforts of Michael Milken, whether corporations or corporate raiders, they were now able to issue their junk bonds to institutions around the world. The bonds paid high interest rates and had a decent track record of avoiding default. Investors kept asking for more. So much more, that Drexel didn't have enough of the bonds to actually sell them. And so it came to pass that the first CDOs were made up of junk bonds.

Drexel collected a diverse pool of bonds from corporations in different industries and put them into a CDO. The investors in that CDO would bear losses on the pool in inverse relation to their place in the capital structure. Drexel got its first CDO deal done and in so doing figured out a way to satiate the demand for its junk bonds without actually underwriting any new ones.

In 1987, Ira Wagner, the man who would eventually run the CDO group at Bear Stearns, was six years out of the Wharton School of business and working in the mortgage securitization department of Drexel. Wagner watched as the first CDO was created at Drexel, though he was not directly involved in that effort. When Drexel went under in 1990, the men and women like Wagner who had helped pioneer its efforts in securitization and CDOs dispersed among various Wall Street firms. While Drexel's CDOs based on junk bonds had an ignominious end, given the crash in the junk bond market in 1990, these securitizers kept the spirit of CDOs alive.

By the mid-1990s, with the economy back on its feet and default rates on junk bonds falling, former employees of Drexel such as Ira Wagner started looking once again at junk bonds as a source of assets for CDOs. Wagner had by this point joined Bear Stearns, where he would remain for the next 12 years, leaving only weeks before the firm collapsed in March 2008. Today, Wagner pursues his passion for photography and playing the cello. But when he joined Bear Stearns in 1996, his mission was to find new things to securitize.

Securitization is often quite helpful for consumers. It expands the availability of credit and it helps provide financing for projects that create jobs. For example, Ira Wagner securitized the future revenues from the films of Dreamworks so the company could raise money to help produce those films. He also helped finance the construction of the Staples Center in Los Angeles by securitizing the future revenue streams the Center would receive from naming rights, corporate sponsors, and leases on luxury suites. And in the late 1990s, he started once again to eye CDOs, a product that, while not popular, had returned from near-death to post 1996 sales of about $10 billion. Most of those CDOs were once again made up of junk bonds, but Wall Street would also throw in some debt from emerging-market countries or loans that were financing leveraged buyouts.

In 1999, Prudential Securities put together the first CDO comprised of another securitization, a *CDO of asset-backed securities (ABSs)*. It was a CDO made up of a diverse set of securitized assets. There were some mortgage securities and some securities backed by assets such as credit card receivables and auto loans. It wouldn't take long for securitizers such as Wagner to start thinking of other asset-backed securities that could be made into CDOs. One early favorite was a CDO made of securities backed by mobile homes and the franchise fees paid to Burger King and McDonald's.

It turns out that those CDOs didn't do so well (is there a pattern here?) and the CDO-makers settled on a new and growing asset class to stand behind their handiwork, residential mortgage-backed securities (RMBSs), particularly ones made up of higher-yielding subprime mortgages. The original idea behind a CDO, to have a diverse group of assets that were not likely to go bad at the same time, had been done away with. Now, the CDO market, which was ballooning in size, was inextricably tied to mortgages and the asset that stood behind a mortgage, a home. Those assets had been doing quite well for many years. Mortgages didn't show many defaults, and as the price of homes moved higher it seemed a pretty sure bet people would be able to keep paying back their mortgages.

In 2003, when Wall Street was just starting to wrest control of the mortgage securitization market from Fannie Mae and Freddie Mac, roughly 43 percent of all CDOs issued featured collateral that was a subprime residential mortgage-backed security. By 2006, 71 percent of all CDOs issued would have those securities as their collateral. CDOs and MBSs were huge fee generators for Wall Street. The growth in CDOs backed by subprime mortgage assets mirrored the growth in Wall Street's share of the mortgage securitization market. And there's a key reason why.

Turning "Crap into Triple-A"

Ann Rutledge, a former analyst at Moody's who rated structured products, is concise in her explanation of how it came to be that many CDOs were given triple-A credit ratings. "There are so many ways to turn something that's crap into triple-A," says Rutledge. "If you just follow the rules without following the spirit of the rules, it's not difficult to do." That willingness of the rating agencies to turn their backs on common sense helps explain one of the era's most toxic concoctions.

By 2005, the subprime frenzy was in full force. Originators were giving out mortgages as fast as they could and Wall Street was securitizing them with equal abandon. This was the time during which the volume of mortgages being purchased at Michael Francis's firm was fast approaching $4 billion a month.

With so many mortgage-backed securities being issued, the banks began to encounter a problem. The bottom of the securitization (or waterfall) was becoming a tougher sell. These BBB and BBB− tranches carried a decent interest rate, but it was not proving good enough to lure buyers. The banks didn't want to stop creating mortgage-backed securities, but they found themselves awash in the riskiest part of the pool that they couldn't sell and didn't want to keep. It was a problem.

They turned to the math geniuses in the CDO group for a solution. That solution was called a *mezzanine CDO*, and it was a piece of financial alchemy the likes of which we may never see again. When Alan Greenspan professes ignorance of the investment merits of CDOs, he is thinking primarily about mezzanine CDOs. When Sylvain Raynes, who rated structured products for Moody's, talks about rating agency analysts being bullied by highly paid investment bankers, and Ann Rutledge talks about turning crap into triple-A, they are talking about mezzanine CDOs.

A mezzanine CDO was constructed from the BBB and BBB– tranches of subprime mortgage-backed securities. One might necessarily assume that such a product, given its component parts, would have a similar credit rating. But that is an assumption only someone who has never worked on Wall Street would make. In fact, the rating agencies were happy to say that as much as 80 percent of a CDO made up of triple-B and triple-B-minus-rated securities made from subprime mortgages was triple-A. It boggles the mind, but it's true.

Ira Wagner says the idea was to combine BBB and BBB– mortgage securities that contained different types of mortgages originated in different years, by different mortgage lenders, from different parts of the country. All that diversity would somehow allow the investment bank to profess that the chances of being paid back on the CDO were markedly better than on the securities from which it was created. It may sound like a strange argument, but somehow the rating agencies bought it.

Hundreds of billions of dollars' worth of this "crap," as Ann Rutledge called it, was unloaded on unsuspecting investors the world over. The CDO business was a global one. The same investors at banks and sovereign wealth funds in China, Asia, the Middle East, and Continental Europe who bought mortgage-backed securities, piled into CDOs. Most of them never bothered to look beyond the triple-A rating on the cover of the mezzanine CDO's prospectus. Even if they had bothered to read the fine print, it's far from clear they would have truly understood the trouble they were buying. It was trouble that Wall Street was more than happy to export so it could keep its mortgage machine humming.

The practitioners of securitization like to refer to the process as a "technology." Talk to any of them for a while and they'll start referring to their technology as though they were responsible for inventing something like the personal computer or Internet search. But after studying the world of securitization in 2006 and 2007, I must admit that it does resemble technology. It reminds me of science fiction movies such as *The Matrix* and *Terminator*, in which technology has outrun humankind's ability to control it.

"Structured finance is a dynamic form of finance," warns Sylvain Raynes. "It is very powerful. Powerful things are dangerous. An airplane is more powerful than a car. It's also more dangerous than a car. So it is regulated more." No such regulation existed that could contain the CDO.

In 2006, $551 billion worth of CDOs were issued, most of which were comprised of subprime mortgage-backed securities. In 2007, when signs of an end to the housing boom were obvious, Wall Street still managed to issue the second largest amount of CDOs ever: $503 billion. At this point, the technology had moved beyond things as improbable as the mezzanine CDO and on to products that truly seem as though they could have been created only by some computer bent on destroying the financial world.

One of them is known as a *synthetic CDO*. I need to explain synthetic CDOs because they are one reason why our banks have lost so much money. But in order to do that, I need to take you on a brief journey into the world of credit default swaps.

From CDS to CDO

A *credit default swap* (CDS) is a form of insurance. It is protection that an investor can buy that guards against the risk that a particular piece of debt will default. The value of a credit default swap rises and falls based on the perceived likelihood that what it is insuring will default. In that sense, it provides a way for holders of the actual debt security to hedge their risk. That's all well and good, but Wall Street loves nothing more than to take a good idea to an extreme that eventually makes it a very bad idea.

Wall Street found credit default swaps to be a very profitable product. At very little cost, a bank or insurance company such as AIG could sell *credit protection* for which it would receive a nice-sized fee, without the need for the institution to set aside much of a reserve in case it actually had to pay off on that credit protection.

The market for credit default swaps is completely unregulated. There are no standards, no capital requirements, and no authority singling out bad actors or keeping track of what has been issued. Even though these products appear to be a form of insurance and might have been regulated at the very least by state insurance administrators, that never happened.

Michael Greenberger, former director of the Division of Trading and Markets at the Commodity Futures Trading Commission, blames former Republican Senator Phil Gramm from Texas for that lack of regulation. In an interview, Mr. Greenberger told me the following story:

> It's Friday night, December 15, 2000. The Presidential and Congressional elections have taken place. Congress is going off for the Christmas recess and ending that Congress. They have before them an 11,000-page Omnibus Appropriation Bill to fund the entire federal government for fiscal year 2001.

> Senator Gramm walks to the floor that night and puts a floor rider on it, a 262-page bill called The Commodity Futures Modernization Act of 2000. And he deregulates these markets. I don't believe anyone in Congress besides Senator Gramm, and sometimes I wonder whether even Senator Gramm, understood what they were doing.

> This was a piece of legislation that was not written by any hand in Congress, either Senators, Congressmen or their staffs. It was written on Wall Street. And six ways from Sunday, it deregulated these markets, not only from federal oversight, but from state oversight as well.

Senator Gramm says his bill *did not* deregulate credit default swaps. In speeches and editorials, he maintains that all the bill did when it came to credit default swaps was provide legal certainty that they were not futures contracts. Beyond that, says the Senator (now a vice chairman of the hobbled Swiss banking giant UBS), the credit default swap remained subject to regulation "just as before based on who issued the swap and the nature of the underlying contracts."

Of course, that was still the key problem. No one was regulating either of those things.

When the CDS market began in the late 1990s, it was most often used by investors to insure against default on a corporate bond that they owned. But credit default swaps held so much more promise for profits than just that. Soon enough, investors could simply buy a credit default swap on a piece of debt that they didn't own, making a bet that that piece of debt (known as a *reference obligation*) would fall in value, sending the credit default swap up in value.

Things only got worse (or better, for those who were selling these things) from there. Consider that AIG, now owned by the U.S. taxpayer, is currently unwinding credit default swaps on $2.7 trillion worth of debt securities, according to the *Washington Post*. At the height of its credit-default-writing frenzy in 2005 and 2006, AIG would sell credit protection on virtually anything. And why not? It had a AAA credit rating and so an extremely low cost for borrowing money and it barely needed to keep anything in reserve for this insurance, which its computer models said it would never need to pay off.

All of this takes us back to the synthetic CDO. By 2005, Wall Street firms were still trying to meet the demand for all the mortgage-related products they had created. But they were running out of ways to do it. CDOs fueled demand for mortgage-backed securities. Mortgage-backed securities fueled demand for mortgages. The problem was that there simply weren't enough mortgages being made to meet the world-wide demand Wall Street had created for CDOs. Or, said another way, they had run out of actual mortgages to package up and sell and so started to create *hypothetical* ones. That's how you get a synthetic CDO.

The synthetic CDO owes its existence to the credit default market. Without CDSs, there would be no synthetic CDOs. That's because a synthetic CDO was created from the credit default swaps that had been written on various tranches of mortgage-backed securities. The buyer of a CDS on a BBB piece of a mortgage securitization is obligated to pay the interest on that piece of the security to whoever wrote them the credit default swap.

A Wall Street firm would aggregate hundreds of credit default swaps written on the different tranches of residential mortgage-backed securities and sell them to investors in a CDO, whose owners would receive the same interest payments as the referenced pieces of the mortgage-backed security. In return, the owners of that CDO would agree to put up money as collateral for the insurance they were providing (the CDS) and would be forced to cough up more money if the credit quality of the referenced mortgage-backed security declined in value.

The best way to explain how a synthetic CDO works is to think of fantasy football. In fantasy football, you choose a player as your reference obligation and your team earns points based on the player's performance. You don't own the player. You have no relationship to the player. But you win and someone else loses if you're betting in fantasy football depending on how your referenced players perform in their games.

In order to create a synthetic CDO, an investment bank would need to find investors who were willing to buy credit protection from it on various tranches of RMBSs. The people in the business of creating securities made from mortgages were now trying to find people to bet that those mortgages would go bad.

Synthetic CDOs had an added bonus for the investment banks. While a *cash CDO* could take months to put together given the need to amass the mortgage-backed securities that would comprise it, a synthetic CDO could be cobbled together in a matter of days if there was enough demand for credit default swaps referencing mortgage-backed securities that already existed. The quicker the deal came together, the quicker Wall Street could book its fees.

Insanity Sets In

It is hard to understate the insanity that seemed to have crept into the CDO market by 2006–2007. Young structurers only a few years out of business school were working 14-hour days and making a million dollars a year to put together CDOs and synthetic CDOs to feed the demand their bosses had created for this product. Having spoken with a few of these now-unemployed people, it's clear that they didn't really understand the bigger picture. Their sole focus was on doing the mathematical work required of them to get the pieces in place to make a CDO and get it the necessary credit rating that would let it sell.

At the same time, a small but growing group of investors who believed the mortgage market was going to collapse (see Chapter 10) were anxiously betting on just that outcome by buying those credit default swaps on RMBSs.

The history of this period has yet to be fully documented. I have done a fair share of reporting and can tell you that many of the participants in this market believe that with the proper examination, significant fraud will be found. One area to examine is the relationship between certain hedge funds and the banks that were creating synthetic CDOs.

In order to create a synthetic CDO, the banks needed to find someone to buy the equity in the deal—that small sliver at the very bottom of the waterfall that would absorb the very first losses from the securitization. A number of funds were willing to buy that equity, not because they believed it would be a good investment, but because by doing so they would insure the creation of the synthetic CDO, giving them the opportunity to bet against an entire pool of RMBS collateral by buying credit default swaps on it.

If anyone ever does look into this, he may want to investigate whether the banks were choosing the best collateral for their CDO investors or were perhaps more mindful of the needs of the hedge funds that were willing to buy the equity of the deal in order to bring it to life. And why would the hedge funds do this? Because even if the equity was a zero, the money they would make by *shorting* all the collateral would more than make up for that loss.

By this point, Wall Street's financial innovation had spawned even more products in the CDO family—products that would eventually help devour the balance sheets of the very banks that created them. In addition to the now-staid CDO and the synthetic CDO, there was also something known as the *CDO-squared*, and its sister, the *synthetic CDO-squared*.

A CDO-squared is a CDO made up not of mortgage-backed securities but of other CDOs. It's just another derivative product of a mortgage even further down the chain. By creating CDO-squareds, the banks were essentially creating demand for CDOs. And as 2006 ended and demand from investors for CDOs began to fall, the banks were nonetheless able to create false demand for the various tranches of a CDO by constructing CDO-squareds.

The allure for an investor came with the yield on these products. A synthetic CDO and a CDO-squared paid a slightly higher yield than a typical CDO, and a synthetic CDO-squared paid still more than that.

Of course, most of the buyers for these works of science fiction had no idea whether they were synthetic or squared or both. They just stupidly bought them.

But talk about *stupid*: Ever wonder how it came to be that the banks that created all these CDOs ended up losing so much money on them? After all, if they were *selling* them to investors, then why did Merrill Lynch or Citigroup end up taking tens of billions of losses on their CDOs? If you've reviewed the write-downs taken by Citi or Merrill or UBS, you have probably noticed the phrase "super-senior tranche of ABS CDOs."

The *super-senior tranche* is another of those make-believe Wall Street terms that don't mean what they imply. In this case, it refers to the part of the CDO with the least-supposed credit risk—even less risk than the triple-A part of the CDO.

By 2006 and 2007, many investors in CDOs didn't feel that the yield on the triple-A part of CDOs was high enough, running as it often did at as little as 20 basis points above U.S. Treasury bonds of the same duration. But the banks really wanted to collect the fees from their CDOs and there was investor interest in the lower-rated parts of the structure. So, the banks invented super-senior by effectively dividing the risk within the triple-A-rated part of the CDO, so the super-senior would get even less interest and the triple-A would now get more. A bank would keep the super-senior tranche, which paid that very low interest rate, on its own balance sheet. While it didn't pay much, the bank's cost of capital was lower still and so there was some money to be made. But most important, by doing all this the bank was able to insure it could sell the rest of the CDO.

The only problem was that in many deals the banks would end up owning as much as 90 percent of the dollar amount. Most CDOs were about one billion dollars in size, which means the banks would keep $900 million in super-senior risk. That can add up quickly.

The banks did try to hedge the risk of owning that part of CDOs. They went to firms like AIG and bought credit default swaps on their own CDOs. But by 2006, even AIG didn't want to insure the super-senior tranche of CDOs. That didn't stop banks like Merrill Lynch from making them anyway and keeping 90 percent of the CDO for themselves, all of it unhedged. After all, it had virtually no risk, right?

Maybe in a different world that would have been true. But in this world, guys like Lou Pacific were giving mortgages to people like Arturo Trevilla. Mortgages that were sold to Wall Street firms such as the one where Michael Francis worked were turned into mortgage-backed securities that guys like Ira Wagner then turned into CDOs. None of these people were bad. They were doing their best to provide for their families. They were all just part of the chain. And where did that chain end? Sometimes it ended in the unlikeliest of places.

Chapter 8

Narvik and Me

Somehow I imagined Narvik, Norway, would all be a lot more pleasant—*Sound-of-Music* pretty with lots of verdant vistas and beautiful people. It just wasn't. In fact, Narvik, a town of 18,000 people 150 miles inside the Arctic Circle, was downright depressing. And not just because the town was battling to stay solvent after gorging itself on CDOs made from what it thought were American mortgages.

Drab architecture and dull concrete give Narvik a "Soviet" feel. That will happen when a place is bombed into the Stone Age. I'm told it was quite a wondrous little port town before the Germans and British laid waste to it in the spring of 1940.

Gray, endless days. A constant chill in the air. It took me four airplane rides and a full 36 hours to get there. This, in the middle of a beautiful summer with my family in Montauk, New York. Not that I'm complaining. I always wanted to see the Arctic. I actually saw a few moose. And it is kind of cool to witness the sun never going down.

I slept surprisingly well in Narvik. My hotel room put me in mind of what it must be like to bunk on a submarine. Very cozy. I watched a lot of the summer Olympics on a tiny TV in the corner of my submarine bunk. The Norwegians have an impressive number of Olympic athletes for a country with only five million people.

Narvik, Norway
Photo courtesy of CNBC.

My documentary crew and I did take one hike, laboring (at least *I* labored) up the main mountain in town. I would have worked up a sweat if it weren't freezing. The winter comes on early in the Arctic. August kind of early. Still, we had a nice beer at the top. It cost $14. Did I mention I have never been anywhere nearly as expensive as Norway?

The mountains and fjords were beautiful, and the people seemed perfectly nice. What few of them are left. That's where Narvik's problems begin. No one under the age of 50 wants to live there anymore. And I can understand why. Before I left Norway, I spent one day walking around Norway's capital, Oslo. It's a whole lot nicer than Narvik.

One would think that Norway, with its huge reserves of capital from all that natural gas it's been pumping out of the North Sea, would be a bit more generous with its struggling municipalities. But apparently the Norwegians are fixated on planning for their collective future. No Ponzi scheme–styled Social Security plan for them. They've got the cash ($400 billion or so in one of the largest sovereign funds) and are holding onto it for dear life. Even if it means their population-losing towns have to get creative with their own finances.

And that's just what Narvik, Norway, did. Which is the reason I spent six days in that gray, chilly, depressing town eating lots of smoked salmon and avoiding *Hvalbiff*, the town's local delicacy, otherwise known as whale meat.

CDOs: An American Export

It's not like CDOs didn't wind up in the coffers of pension funds or municipalities all over the United States. But that's to be expected. The thing about CDOs was just how far-and-wide the bankers who created them were willing to travel to peddle them. If they made it to Narvik, Norway, that pretty much makes the point. The entire world was enlisted to help fund mortgages for people who were buying homes in the United States.

Of course, the people in Narvik who decided to buy CDOs had no idea what they were buying—only that they had a triple-A rating. And even that, it turns out, is in question.

What Narvik was trying to do was get itself a little more revenue each year so that it would not be forced to cut back on the services its residents expected despite their diminishing numbers. Narvik had been climbing that financial hill for years. Attempting to get a bit more return on its tax revenues, it relied on the services of a Norwegian brokerage firm known as Terra Securities to provide the financial advice to eke out a slightly larger investment return each year.

At first, on advice from Terra, Narvik's Town Council invested in the stocks of major Norwegian companies and obligations of other Norwegian municipalities. But by 2005, Narvik's brokers at Terra had a new idea. They advised the Town Council to borrow money secured by the future tax revenues that would come from the town's hydroelectric plants (lots of waterfalls in the Arctic) and then take that borrowed money and find a security that would bring a higher yield than what the town was paying on its borrowings.

It was an easy plan. Narvik wasn't swinging for the fences. It was merely going to post a small gain every year between what it was paying on its borrowed money (Norwegian municipalities can borrow quite cheaply) and what it would earn from the ultra-safe triple-A-rated securities that Terra would tell it to purchase.

In the spring of 2005, Terra discovered those ultra-safe securities. It seems the men from Terra had met some men from Citigroup who interested them in a safe, structured product coming out of the United States that paid interest at roughly 1 percent above LIBOR, a widely used reference rate that closely tracks the Federal Funds rate.

Narvik bought something called a *managed portfolio linked repackaging CDO*. It wasn't a true CDO, which would have been scary enough. Even worse, it was a synthetic CDO—one of those CDOs comprised of the proceeds from credit default swaps that had been written on a portfolio of "referenced" securities. I realize that's difficult to understand, even with my explanation from Chapter 7. And I am almost certain that to this day no one in Narvik has any understanding of the investments that sunk their town. To make matters worse, the securities Narvik bought, while investment grade, were not triple-A rated, but of a lesser rating. They would absorb losses far quicker than the triple-A piece of the structured product.

When I interviewed Narvik's lawyer, Ulf Larsen, who is representing it and the seven other Norwegian municipalities that bought these synthetic CDOs, he kept referring to "triggers" that forced Narvik to keep forking money over to Citigroup. He was unsure of how those triggers worked or why Narvik was forced to cough up the money. The triggers were a part of the mechanism of a synthetic CDO. As the value of the securities on which the credit protection had been sold declined (due in part to downgrades from the rating agencies), those who were buying that protection exercised their right to demand more collateral. If you've bought insurance on something and it looks like you're going to need to collect, you want to make sure the money is there to take.

Narvik made good on two of its trigger payments and then gave up. By that time, the town had blown through more than $15 million. I know it doesn't seem like much money, but for Narvik it was a quarter of its annual budget.

Karen Kuvaas, Mayor of Narvik
Photo courtesy of CNBC.

Karen Kuvaas is the mayor of Narvik, Norway. With blonde hair, blue eyes, and tanned and well-worn skin, she looks just as one might expect a Norwegian lady to appear. When I interviewed her at her office, Kuvaas had just returned from a skiing trip in Austria (even with their town in deep trouble, people in Norway have a pretty nice standard of living). She's a soft-spoken, middle-aged politician who inherited the job from the guy who authorized Terra to buy those CDOs.

Kuvaas seems mildly entertained by the notion that her tiny town has become emblematic of Wall Street's endless search for investors willing to buy its crap. But she is also a mayor dealing with a crisis. Narvik is running out of money and services are getting cut back rapidly.

In the week I was there, classrooms at the local schools were being combined, personnel at the local nursing home was being reduced, and the town's one major (manmade) tourist attraction, a museum dedicated to the historic World War II battle of Narvik, was preparing to close for good. It's too bad. It was a pretty cool museum, filled with many of the weapons the Nazis hid in the Narvik hills as they defended

Taking a Walk with Narvik's Mayor, Karen Kuvaas
Photo courtesy of CNBC.

their position. Narvik is one of the northernmost warm-water ports in the world and it was the place from where the Germans were able to send all the iron ore they were mining in Sweden back home so it could be made into the stuff that wound up in Narvik's museum: tanks, artillery, bullets, and any other instrument of war one can think of.

The people of Narvik have no idea how their town lost its money, but they are painfully aware of its effects. Everywhere my crew and I went in the town, people seemed to know why we were there. "They don't understand how their politicians and administrators could be so stupid," says Kuvaas.

Kuvaas may not have been mayor when the town agreed to its ill-fated deal, but she was on the Town Council. She admits Narvik's leaders had no clue as to what they were buying, only that Terra had been a good advisor to the town in the past and that Citigroup was a name they all recognized.

Kuvaas and the rest of the town's elected officials only came to realize what they had done well after the securities had been purchased.

Narvik's Main Tourist Attraction, a Museum Devoted to the Battle of Narvik, Was Forced to Shut Down
Photo courtesy of CNBC.

In the first nine months that they owned the CDOs, they continued to pay the promised interest without a need for Narvik to put up more money. But even after the first trigger payment was made, Kuvaas says the town's advisors from Terra told them not to worry.

Kuvaas recalls a presentation to the Town Council in which its advisors from Terra assured them that everything would be fine. Kuvaas says that most of her fellow Council members were confused by a series of boxes their advisors had drawn to try to illustrate the investment the town had undertaken. "I would say it was rather confusing and there were few persons in the City Council who understood the whole thing. But I think many of us got anxious and suspicious because we didn't understand much about the boxes."

Ulf Larsen is suing Citigroup, and not Terra, on behalf of Narvik and the other Norwegian municipalities that put up about a quarter of a billion dollars to buy Citigroup's synthetic CDOs. Terra went bankrupt not long after it brokered the synthetic CDO deal to Narvik.

Larsen contends that not only did the Town Council in Narvik have no idea what it was buying, but its brokers at Terra also never fully understood what a CDO was and how it worked. Larsen also admits he didn't fully understand what his clients purchased. That's evident from the fact that during our entire interview he never once referred to the CDOs as having been synthetic, nor could he explain to me how and why these mysterious triggers actually worked or why they existed in the first place.

Larsen did know that selling CDOs, synthetic or otherwise, brought big fees for Terra. Fees that he claims were sometimes as much as 10 percent of a deal. And he claims he will prove in court that Citigroup was also well aware of the ultimate buyers of its handiwork. He brandished an agenda for a seminar in London held by Citigroup that brokers from Terra attended. The daylong program included an update on the credit markets from Matt King, the 20-something head of Global Credit Strategy at Citigroup. While King would become quite pessimistic on the state of the credit markets by the spring of 2008, it's far from clear that that was his message in November 2006 when he gave a briefing to brokers from Terra.

Larsen alleges that, given its meetings with the brokers from Terra, Citigroup must have been aware of who was buying the CDOs from Terra and how completely inappropriate those securities were for a Norwegian municipality. At this writing, that will be for a court in London to decide.

The Truth Revealed—But Does It Matter?

If only our story ended there. In researching Narvik's CDOs for this book, I found that they were not synthetic CDOs comprised of credit default swaps written on mortgage-backed securities, but CDOs made up of credit default swaps written on U.S. corporate and municipal debt. The town had not invested in the U.S. mortgage market.

We went to Narvik because dozens of reports from news organizations such as the *New York Times*, not to mention the endless coverage of the Norwegian press, maintained the town had lost its money from

CDOs tied to the U.S housing market. News crews from as far away as Australia traveled to Narvik and filed reports saying the same thing. I can't really blame them. They were taking the mayor's word for it and she was relying on their lawyer who was relying on his "experts" to tell him what was in those CDOs. None of them ever figured it out. At least not until we called and told them.

It didn't matter. When the credit crisis began in the summer of 2007, anything with the initials CDO was a goner, including the junk that Narvik bought into, even if it wasn't directly connected to the U.S. housing market.

Narvik, like other investors around the world, would learn never to trust Wall Street again. But before that day came, Wall Street's mortgage machine was raking in huge profits. Just ask Merrill Lynch.

Chapter 9

Mortgaging Merrill's Future

And the man played golf. Alone. Stan O'Neal, chairman and CEO of Merrill Lynch, played at least 13 rounds of golf between August 12 and September 30, 2007. He played at clubs such as Shinnecock Hills in Southampton, New York; Vineyard Golf Club in Martha's Vineyard; the Purchase Country Club in Purchase, New York; and Waccabuc Country Club in Upstate New York. And almost every time O'Neal played, he played alone.

I'm not telling you this to pick on Stan O'Neal. CEOs are allowed to golf, especially on weekends at the end of the summer. To judge from his USGA Handicap Index History, O'Neal is quite a proficient golfer, typically producing scores in the mid-to-low eighties. It's nice to see evidence of someone who not only enjoys a sport, but plays it well.

What's weird about it all is that while Stan O'Neal was playing golf, the company he had run with an iron fist for the last five years was about to implode. It's hard to imagine what was going through O'Neal's mind as he traversed the links in the late summer days of 2007. Was he clearing his thoughts to try to fashion a plan for Merrill's resurgence? Was he focused on understanding the roots of the problems his storied 93-year-old firm was only beginning to acknowledge? Was he thinking about his next shot?

After speaking to colleagues of O'Neal's who spent time with him during those August and September days, I think O'Neal already knew the end was near. He knew he might soon lose his job and may have started to understand that Merrill itself could be lost as well. Why was Stan O'Neal golfing alone while the flames of an emerging fire were beginning to engulf his firm? Perhaps because it was too late for him to do anything else.

O'Neal is a notoriously private person. In the years he ran Merrill, I never met or interviewed him even once and he declines to speak with me to this day. And if you're wondering whether that's a rare occurrence, in my case it is. Given how long I've been covering Wall Street, I have typically managed to meet, if not get to know, all the heads of the major firms that do business there, including the man who preceded O'Neal as Merrill's CEO, David Komansky.

O'Neal seemed to have particular antipathy for CNBC. I've never been certain why. But I do know that upon his ascension to the position of CEO, he had our network removed from the television programming piped in via computer to the firm's 16,000 or so brokers.

Climbing Out of Poverty

O'Neal's is a great American story. "Whatever I have achieved in life has been the result of the unique combination of luck, hard work and opportunity that can only exist in this country," O'Neal has said. His grandfather was born into slavery in 1861. Young Stan attended a one-room schoolhouse in a small town in rural Alabama. It served students from grades one through six, all taught by the same teacher. His home, like his school, had no indoor plumbing or running water.

When O'Neal was 13 years old, his family moved to Atlanta so that his father could take a job as an assembly worker at a General Motors plant. O'Neal lived in a federal housing project, but over time his parents were able to save some money and his family moved into a home of their own. "Watching my parents work and save to afford their home gave me an appreciation of the unique pride and satisfaction that comes with home ownership," O'Neal told a congressional panel in March 2008. Maybe that's why Merrill became the mother of all mortgage companies.

O'Neal would also go on to work at a GM assembly plant to help pay for his education. He attended the General Motors Institute in Michigan and went on to receive an MBA from the Harvard Business School. After graduating from Harvard, O'Neal went to work full time for GM and rose to become a director in the company's Treasury division. He joined Merrill in 1987 and quickly moved up. He became CFO in 1998, president in 2001, and CEO in 2002. It was an amazing climb through one of the toughest of corporate ladders, made all the more intriguing because of O'Neal's incredibly humble origins.

You would have to want to root for a guy like Stan O'Neal even if he would never talk to you—even if he removed any trace of your network from his firm. Even if he was not a nice guy, you would simply have to hope, given where he came from and what he did to get where he was, that he succeeded.

In fact, that's just what it appeared O'Neal was doing. Under the leadership of Stan O'Neal, business at Merrill seemed to be going really well. Known as a numbers guy, O'Neal took over from the avuncular Komansky with the expectation that the company would start keeping a closer eye on costs. I distinctly remember many a conversation with some of the firm's investment bankers in which they nervously wondered whether O'Neal would deal their hefty compensation a death blow.

O'Neal did plenty to add to that reputation when, upon taking control of the company, he summarily dismissed many of Komansky's loyalists and seemed bent on removing anyone over the age of 50 from the ranks of upper management. In a comment that was more prophetic at the time than I could ever have imagined, a senior banker at Merrill admitted that while the firm's upper ranks were "bloated" it wasn't necessary to throw everyone out. He angrily dismissed O'Neal as naïve and said that "Stan has surrounded himself with thugs who don't know the business." He wondered whether O'Neal might one day be hurt by having no one in senior management who was willing to challenge his decisions.

A Strong Start

O'Neal never had great regard for investment bankers, believing they were commodity players who garnered their value from the franchise they inherited and the balance sheet they had to offer clients. One senior banker at the firm told me back in 2002 that it was clear O'Neal was no fan of investment banking and didn't much care if Merrill was first, second, or third in the closely watched ranking of who was doing the most deals. All he was interested in, said this banker, was reducing costs at the investment bank to the point where it generated a good return. But after lots of tough talk at the beginning of his reign as CEO, O'Neal never made good on his threats to start paying all those investment bankers no more than $400,000 a year. Instead, he largely left them alone.

Still, the man from Alabama seemed to be running a tight ship. With few exceptions, the quarterly earnings progression of Merrill under his watch was a positive one. The firm's revenues rose sharply from 2002 until 2006 and so did its profits.

With each quarter's new record profits, I would dutifully report Merrill's success, making sure to mention that O'Neal was delivering on his promise to grow revenues while also increasing the firm's profit margin and closely watched return on equity (the profit generated by a company from the money shareholders have invested). Companies typically put out a press release detailing their earnings results and accompany that with a conference call with investors that members of the press can listen to. At the end of every earnings press release, Merrill would list its noncompensation expenses, a report card for how O'Neal was doing in his supposed focus on containing the cost of things such as postal expenditures, office rents, and telecommunications spending.

I've thought a lot about my reporting on Merrill's earnings from that period, particularly during the years of 2005 and 2006, when the firm seemed to be printing money and its stock price soared from the mid-twenties to almost $100 a share. What I have realized is how little I knew of what was driving the firm's earnings in those years.

I talked to plenty of people at Merrill, from brokers to bankers to a handful of senior management. I had many friends at the firm and, to this day, still have my brokerage account at Merrill (it's pretty boring stuff since I can't invest in individual stocks or corporate bonds). Our conversations would often traverse subjects like mergers and acquisitions, the growth of private equity, the sagacity of extending covenant-free levered loans for leveraged buyouts, and the state of the equity and bond markets. But during all those years and all those conversations, no one ever mentioned the word *mortgages*. It simply never came up. And I regret that I didn't know enough to ever ask.

The Secret Weapon

In all those quarterly earnings releases detailing the firm's growing success under O'Neal, one would be hard pressed to find the word *mortgage*. I've looked. While the business of buying, securitizing, and selling mortgages had become the biggest engine of its incredible growth, the firm never mentioned that fact. I certainly had no idea that Merrill was a huge mortgage machine masquerading as an investment bank. And neither did many of its employees.

Talk to brokers or investment bankers at the firm and they'll tell you they had no idea what Merrill was doing in the mortgage business. Some may have vaguely recalled the purchase of the mortgage lender First Franklin for $1.3 billion in late 2006 and everyone knew that Merrill's Fixed Income unit was going gangbusters. But fixed income was a broadly based business encompassing a multitude of products usually associated with corporate bonds.

Merrill wasn't talking about mortgage-backed securities or collateralized debt obligations (CDOs) in its earnings releases or in the numbers that accompanied them. Figuring out just how big a part of Merrill's earnings those products had become would have been nearly impossible from looking at Merrill's revenues, because all of the Fixed Income division's revenues were reported as part of another business known as Fixed Income Currencies and Commodities, which itself was reported as a part of the revenues of the giant Global Markets and Investment Banking division.

If you took the trouble to read the company's quarterly earnings filings with the Securities and Exchange Commission from 2005 or 2006, you would finally find evidence that underwriting and securitizing mortgages was a part of Merrill's business. But having done that, you still would have been hard pressed to understand what role that activity played in the firm's profitability.

A quick look at the quarterly filing for the period ending September 29, 2006, shows clearly enough that securitization of mortgages and other assets was increasing markedly from $64.5 billion for the nine-month period ending September 29, 2005, to $91.5 billion for the same nine-month period a year later. But without a deeper knowledge of Merrill's business, an investor or reporter might still have missed the significance of that increase. And there was no mention in any way of the words that would come back to haunt this once-proud company: *collateralized debt obligation.* Merrill wasn't alone in its omission of key details regarding its profitability. The same was true of many of the major Wall Street firm's that were gorging themselves on all those mortgages being made by our friends from Irvine, California.

Whether it was Citigroup, Bear Stearns, Morgan Stanley, UBS, or Goldman Sachs, if you were searching for evidence of a huge new business at these firms you would not have found it in their public statements. And I can tell you first-hand that aside from the small group of employees who worked at these firms buying mortgages and structuring products made out of them, no one had any idea what a center for profits the business had become.

Even Lehman Brothers, the first firm on Wall Street to delve deeply into the mortgage business, seemed to shy away from talking about it. A quick reading of any of the firm's earnings press releases from the period of 2005 and 2006 does not yield any reference to the origination or securitization of residential mortgages. It's lumped in with the firm's results from its Capital Markets division.

Lehman did provide much greater detail of its prowess in the origination and securitization of mortgages in its quarterly earnings filings with the SEC (clearly, it pays to read filings rather than earnings press releases). There we find that Lehman securitized $146 billion worth of residential mortgage loans in 2006, up from $133 billion in 2005 and $101 billion in 2004.

The year 2006 was Lehman's best ever as a public company, despite a noted slowdown in its residential mortgage business as housing prices began to flatten. In 2006, Lehman Brothers earned $4 billion, a 66 percent increase from its 2004 earnings of $2.4 billion. Lehman was certainly advising on more than its share of mergers and acquisitions and it was a fierce competitor when it came to underwriting the sale of stock and bonds. But it was the mortgage boom that had been nicest to Lehman and to its management. The firm's CEO, Richard Fuld, pulled down $28 million in compensation in 2006. Although 75 percent of it was in Lehman stock, Fuld didn't really need to worry. He was already an enormously wealthy man, having been plied with options and stock in addition to lucrative cash bonuses for years. In 2006, his hoard of exercisable stock options alone was worth $100 million.

Lehman wasn't alone in the record books. The year 2006 was also the most profitable in Merrill's long history. It earned $7.6 billion for the year, 49 percent more than it did the year before. Its revenues were also a record $32.7 billion and its return on average common equity was 21.3 percent, also up sharply from the previous year. Even without the supercharging of its earnings from its business in the mortgage arena, 2006 would have been a very good year for Merrill. Its stockbrokers were doing strong business, its investment management partnership with Blackrock looked like a home run, and its investment bankers were advising on and financing plenty of deals. Still, it was the fees from Fixed Income that drove the record profitability, and, within that unit, it was the fees from mortgage securitizations, still growing as a business, that led the way.

Raking It In

Stan O'Neal was paid $48 million in 2006. Dow Kim, the man who led Merrill's mortgage business, pulled down $37 million in 2006. More than half of their compensation came in the form of stock, which would vest over time. But O'Neal, Kim, and their many lieutenants also took home tens of millions in cold, hard cash.

The same type of bounty was being awarded in the mortgage businesses up and down Wall Street. "A lot of people were getting paid a lot of money," recalls mortgage banker Michael Francis. Francis had already been promoted, but his boss was having him set his sights on the riches that might one day be his. "I remember him saying, 'Wait till you have your first payday of $5 million. That's your next goal.'"

It's always been about the money when it comes to Wall Street. People aren't working there so they can cure cancer. But in all the years I've been following finance, I've never quite come to terms with the lavish compensation that is bestowed on many of those who work there. I have tried. It's only money, after all. It is not a precursor to happiness. Still, I have always found it maddening when people who are merely mediocre at their jobs are paid like kings—and on Wall Street that became the rule, rather than the exception.

Yes, Wall Street has always paid its workers well. But there was a time, not so long ago, when it was only the stars who could command compensation that made them instant multimillionaires. Back when I started covering finance, there were a handful of star bankers and traders and money managers who brought home stunning sums. Even *that* never made sense, but at least one could argue they were the best of the best, the franchise players, who in delivering the lion's share of the profits deserved an outsized reward.

As the business of finance became global and began to encompass so many different types of investment products, Wall Street vastly increased in size. With all those people chasing after riches, Wall Street seemed to democratize its lavish compensation structure. You no longer needed to be a star to become rich. Now, almost everyone, even the most junior of professionals, was deserving of at least half a million dollars a year. And if you avoided any major pitfalls, after a few years, your compensation could easily be in the seven figures.

In 2006, Merrill paid out $17 billion in compensation and benefits to its 56,200 employees. That's an average of $302,491 per person and that average includes every secretary, mailroom worker, and switchboard operator in the joint. Clearly, they weren't making over $300,000 a year. Nor, for that matter, were plenty of the firm's bread-and-butter employees—its stockbrokers (they prefer *financial advisors*).

Ten years earlier, Merrill had paid its then-49,800 workers an average of $134,000 a year ($6.7 billion in compensation and benefits). That year, 1996, was a very good one for the firm. See what I mean by democratization? This is an apples-to-apples comparison of compensation. Yes, I know there was inflation, but for the 10 years between January 1997 and January 2007, inflation adds up to 27 percent, not the 125 percent increase in compensation that Merrill paid its workers.

As for the top five executives and their pay in 2006 versus 1996, the discrepancy boggles the mind. According to Merrill's proxy on compensation for 1996, it paid its top five executives a total of $32 million in cash and stock, which amounted to a bit less than half a percent of all the compensation it paid that year. Ten years later, Merrill's proxy detailing compensation for 2006 shows that the top five earners at the firm were paid a total of $172 million. Compensation for the men who led Merrill had increased by 437 percent over 10 years and amounted to a bit more than 1 percent of the firm's total compensation. Another way to look at it: The top one-thousandth of the firm's employees got 1 percent of its money.

Executive compensation on Wall Street and in corporate America in general has been a touchy subject for the past few years and companies have gone to great lengths to explain their methodology for paying our corporate leaders with such munificence.

Merrill's proxy for 2006 provides great detail on the analysis undertaken by the firm's Management Development and Compensation Committee (MDCC) as it figured out what sums to bestow upon its leadership. The MDCC explained that Merrill's 26 percent increase in revenues in 2006 over the year previous "significantly exceeded targeted growth." The MDCC also pointed out that the 44 percent increase in operating earnings for the year was near the top of the Peer Group "with a year-over-year improvement in the Company's share of overall Peer Group Pre-Tax Profit."

The MDCC reserved its highest praise for Stan O'Neal and his team when it came to the subject of return on equity (ROE):

In its discussion of ROE performance, the MDCC focused on the importance of this measure, which had been identified as a high priority for the CEO and the members of executive management. They noted that the improvement had been driven substantially by the achievement of record earnings of $7.6 billion (on an operating basis), which represented a 48 percent increase over the previous year's record. The Committee also noted that these record results reflected solid execution around several specific growth imperatives outlined to the Board over the past three years.

In other words, Stan O'Neal and his team deserved their $172 million because they delivered in every area of importance, especially when it came to the 21.6 percent return Merrill generated on its equity, always a key measurement in the financial services industry.

Remember the $32 million that David Komansky and his team earned back in 1996? What, you might ask, was Merrill's ROE back then? It was 26.8 percent. In fact, in that same year, Komansky steered Merrill to a 47.5 percent increase in net income (virtually identical to 2006's earnings increase) and had taken the ROE from 20.1 percent in 1995 to the far higher 26.8 percent. It was by all measurements a great year and one can imagine Komansky was quite happy with his windfall. Ten years later, Stan O'Neal would fail to outdo Komansky when it came to ROE, but left him standing at the starting line when it came to compensation.

Taking Big Risks

Thirty years ago, most of the firms on Wall Street were partnerships. The "equity" that I keep referring to was owned by a firm's partners. It was their hard-earned money and they made sure it was being used wisely. When David Komansky started as a stockbroker at Merrill in 1968, it was still a partnership. In a partnership, one didn't take risk without everyone knowing about it and understanding it. There was simply too much at stake.

These days, all the major firms that do business in finance are public companies. Their equity is owned by their public shareholders. The managements of these companies would certainly have their public shareholders believe they guard that equity as carefully as they did when they were private partnerships. Interestingly, one of the major strategic objectives that Merrill's board of directors cited as having been accomplished in 2006 was its "oversight of the balance sheet." They wanted their owners to know they were on the lookout for anything that could threaten their equity.

But I am forced to wonder about that stewardship because of another measurement at Merrill that kept going up: its *leverage ratio*. This is a simple measurement that places the assets owned by the firm as the numerator and the equity of the firm as the denominator. At the end of 2006, Merrill had assets (money it was owed) of $841 billion and equity (its own money that would cushion any losses from those assets) of $42 billion. Its balance sheet was levered to 20 times the size of its equity.

With each passing month in 2005 and 2006, Merrill's assets increased in size and its leverage ratio increased as well. That is one way to measure risk on a balance sheet, but it doesn't give a clear picture of that risk. If all the assets were U.S. Treasury bonds, then there would be little reason to worry about being paid back. But when some of those assets are subprime mortgages extended in 2005 and 2006 or securities comprising those mortgages, there may be cause for concern.

As Merrill headed into 2007, it had record earnings, a strong stock price, well-paid executives, a confident board of directors, and a mission to get even bigger in the one area that had been so instrumental to all its success: mortgages. It wanted to originate more mortgages, buy more mortgages, package more mortgages into securities, and package more of those securities into CDOs. And of course, it wanted to sell those securities and CDOs as fast as it possibly could, because that's where the money was. It was also happy to keep increasing the leverage on its balance sheet as its assets ballooned past $1 trillion, driven by the addition of all those mortgages.

You might not have learned much about Merrill's growing mortgage machine if you had read its press releases and SEC filings from 2006. But its annual report for that year did give some hints at what was to come—that is, if you made it to page 32:

> We also enhanced our structured finance business with three strategic transactions in the U.S., United Kingdom and South Korea that we expect to provide additional sources of origination and servicing for our non-prime mortgage-backed securitization and trading platform. Within FICC (Fixed Income,

Currencies and Commodities), on September 5, 2006, we announced an agreement to acquire the First Franklin mortgage origination franchise and related servicing platform from National City Corporation. We expect First Franklin to accelerate our vertical integration in mortgages.

And finally there was this: a description of its efforts in residential mortgage lending that gave some insight into the risks Merrill was taking on as it plunged deeper and deeper into the business of home lending:

We originate and purchase residential mortgage loans, certain of which include features that may result in additional credit risk when compared to more traditional types of mortgages.[...] These loans are predominantly extended to high credit quality borrowers and include:

- Loans where the borrower is subject to payment increases over the life of the loan.
- Interest-only loans where the borrower makes no principal payments on the loan during an initial period and is required to make both interest and principal payments either during the later stages of the loan or in one lump sum at maturity. These loans therefore require the borrower to make larger payments later in the life of the loans if the loans are not otherwise repaid through a refinancing or sale of the property.
- Loans with low rates early in the loan term.
- High LTV ratio loans where the principal amount of the loan is greater than 80 percent of the value of the mortgaged property and the borrower is not required to obtain private mortgage insurance ("PMI"), and/or loans where a mortgage and home equity loan are simultaneously established for the same property. Under our policy, the maximum LTV ratio for originated residential mortgages with no PMI or other security is 95 percent.

We do not currently originate or purchase residential mortgage loans that allow for minimum monthly payments less than the interest accrued on the loan (i.e., negative amortizing loans) or option adjustable rate mortgages.

There it was, laid out in black-and-white. But was it? Yes, Merrill laid out the risks it was taking as it extended its reach into the mortgage market by buying and originating the *affordability products* that had become ubiquitous in the mortgage market. But it did leave out two key risk factors: What would happen to Merrill's efforts if home prices started to go down? And what would happen if the market for the mortgage-backed securities and CDOs that Merrill was feverishly producing from all those mortgages dried up?

Stan O'Neal had spent over 20 years at Merrill Lynch and taken over as CEO in 2002 with an expectation he would increase the company's profitability through cost cutting and efficiency. He didn't do it. Instead, O'Neal had increased profitability by having Merrill take on more and more risk. The firm dove headlong into a mortgage market that was poised to collapse. As 2007 moved along, Merrill's assets equaled more than 27 times its equity, meaning that even a 4 percent decline in the value of those assets would erase all of its capital. But could that possibly happen?

As he played golf at the end of a long summer in 2007, Stan O'Neal knew the answer.

Chapter 10

A House of Cards

Kyle Bass once drove his car 191 miles per hour on a freeway in Dallas, Texas. I know, because I was in the passenger seat. If you're wondering what that looks like, I can't really tell you because I had my eyes closed for most of it. But I did catch a look at the speedometer. The wind gets very loud when you're going 191 miles per hour. My wife wasn't happy about it, but given that I'd survived, all she did was ask that I not drive with Bass again.

Bass doesn't drive that fast anymore. He's got his limited partners to think of, not to mention a lovely family. But back then, when he was a successful institutional salesman at Bear Stearns and later at Legg Mason, Bass liked speed. He still likes to take risks. He was once a competitive diver and will still jump (with many twists and turns) off the occasional cliff. He also likes to get dropped off by helicopter to ski on remote parts of mountains.

And then there was that time he bet the U.S. housing market was built on suspect financing and would soon come tumbling down.

Kyle Bass
Photo courtesy of CNBC.

Digging for Gold

I first met Bass in the mid-1990s. I had a source in the office where he worked who introduced us over the phone one day and thought we might be able to help each other. Bass was a young, aggressive institutional salesman at Bear Stearns who serviced the then-rarefied world of hedge fund managers. Bass took his job further than most institutional salesmen, who typically confined their research to reading the analyst reports spit out by their firms and reciting them to clients. Bass liked to do a lot of research when it came to investing. He liked to make phone calls, read documents, make unscheduled visits to companies, and occasionally hire private detectives, too. That's because Bass's chosen line of work when it came to investing was on the so-called *short* side. A *short seller* borrows shares of a company and sells them, hoping to profit by buying back those shares at a lower price.

Short selling is a dangerous business. Even when you're right, a stock can only go to zero, but when you're wrong, the downside is limitless because stocks can go up and up and up. Bass certainly made his share of long-term investments in companies, but where he shone was when it came to betting against a corporation. He would do his research and then share it with his hedge fund clients, in the hopes they would like the idea and trade through him (that's how he got paid).

In the mid-to-late 1990s, Bass and I used to compare notes on a variety of frauds that hit Wall Street. For whatever reason, it was a period in which there was a proliferation of what are often called *promotes*. In a well-choreographed series of moves, shady management teams would set out to entice investors with the alluring prospects for their companies, typically, but not always, in the natural resources area. One key to uncovering these frauds was in digging up the background of managements or initial shareholders, many of whom had partaken in similar schemes in years past. Another requirement was to debunk the claims those managements had made, whether they'd be a gold find, an oil find, or a technological breakthrough that held the promise of rich reward.

Bass was always good at digging, and so he and I would occasionally find ourselves sharing information as we tried to track down a fraud. Short sellers and the press often have a symbiotic relationship and one that I would argue is entirely positive for investors. I never once reported something Bass told me without first verifying its accuracy, but he helped me to uncover fraudulent companies (or legitimate ones that had overstated their prospects) and that was a help to many investors who sold before the inevitable collapse in their share price.

Not that there aren't times when Bass is wrong. Like any investor, he's been wrong plenty. But one of the few benefits of getting old is experience, and Bass's willingness to learn from his mistakes and test whatever thesis he may have with those who think otherwise contributes to his insight as an investor.

Short sellers have been demonized during the financial crisis. The practice was even banned for a few weeks in the fall of 2008 in the shares of hundreds of companies. Many of the leaders of our nation's financial services firms have blamed short sellers for driving their stocks ever lower.

Certainly, there are participants in the market who spread negative rumors in hopes of benefiting from those rumors as stocks decline.

And there are also those who, in these perilous times, have used the credit markets to try to undermine confidence in a company, while also shorting its stock. Unscrupulous short sellers are to be avoided in the same way that investors who spread falsely positive stories regarding companies should also be shunned. It's not hard to do. Typically, these people are not that bright and so rarely make arguments with great merit. All it takes to debunk them is a little bit of reporting.

True short sellers, like Kyle Bass, should be lauded by investors. In an era when the Securities and Exchange Commission has shown time and again that it is incapable of combating fraud, short sellers help play the role of market policeman. And even when it comes to perfectly legitimate companies, it is not a bad thing to have a group of people who question the invariably rosy forecasts offered up by those corporations.

These days, it's all too easy to be cynical when it comes to the workings of finance, but Bass seems to have been born that way, growing up as a middle-class kid in Florida and Texas. He and I first met when we were investigating the financials of a company called Arakis Energy, whose shares had soared on its prospects for drilling for oil in Sudan. Arakis claimed it had lined up $750 million to finance that drilling, but short sellers like Bass were wary of the deal and questioned whether the money was real. They were right. The financing fell through and Arakis's share price quickly collapsed.

One of my favorite frauds of all time was Bre-X Minerals, a Canadian company that claimed it had made a major gold find in the jungles of Borneo (Indonesia). Bass, like many other short sellers, spent lots of time trying to verify the company's claims, which, given the location of the mining site, was difficult to do. Wall Street piled into this company's shares, sending its value as high as $4 billion, though not an ounce of gold had been produced from the Busang mine, whose prospects for delivering vast quantities of gold were "verified" in geological tests that Bre-X was happy to share with investors.

The problems at Bre-X began when the company's chief geologist "fell" out of a helicopter over the jungles of Borneo. Things unraveled pretty quickly after that. It turns out Mark Twain was right: A goldmine really is a "hole in the ground with a liar on top." Bre-X's geological samples from the Busang mine had been faked. They had been salted with gold taken from somewhere else. The stock soon collapsed.

Building a Case

Bass had spent 14 years questioning the claims of companies like Bre-X and Arakis before he set out on his own by founding a hedge fund in the early days of 2006. It was the height of the greatest housing boom in U.S. history, and, given his penchant for questioning the closely held views of the many, it seems natural that Bass would be given to wonder whether it was an immutable law of the markets that housing prices would never decline on a national basis. As he opened his modestly sized hedge fund, Hayman Capital Partners, Bass decided to focus on the housing boom and everything that had made it possible. And the first thing Bass found was just how easy it had become to buy a house.

"Every single crisis in financial market history has always been caused by free or easy credit. All the way back to the tulip bulbs in Holland," explains Bass. "When you looked at the housing market, you'd find that people were borrowing 100 percent of the money for a home and speculating for free. So, clearly, it was worth looking into."

It wasn't a big secret that home prices had been escalating at a rapid rate all over the country and that a new profession of "home flipping" had been created in the hottest markets of California, Florida, Arizona, and Nevada. After all, when there are a slew of primetime television shows devoted to buying or renovating a home, it's not a stretch to speculate there might be a housing bubble.

It would take months before Bass would understand the true secret of that bubble: People were buying homes they couldn't afford with mortgages they could not pay back. His journey into the mortgage maelstrom would eventually take him from Wall Street to Washington, D.C., to the Inland Empire of California, but in the early days of his research it was three simple facts that Bass latched onto as he developed his thesis.

The first was that the historical relationship between housing prices and income had gone out of whack. For more than 20 years, the median price of a home had represented roughly three years' worth of the median national household income. Incomes and housing prices rose at the same rate. "For the last fifty years, those two lines have been parallel to one another," explains Bass. "But after Greenspan's interest rate cuts in 2001 and 2002, you started to see the average home price in the United States go up not one-and-a-half percent per year after inflation, but six to eight percent a year for the next four years."

Now home prices were running nationally at four-and-a-half times household income, and, in markets like Orange County, California, home prices had hit an incredible 10 times household income. "So we were eight to nine standard deviations from the mean of that historic relationship between median income and home price. And either incomes had to double or home prices had to drop 35 percent to make the relationship work again," explains Bass.

Another fact Bass discovered made him think he'd better figure out this potential trade fast. The number of unsold homes in the United States was approaching a record four million. "If you look at the historic data, inventory of four million homes is unprecedented. So that's what actually sped up my research, because it led me to believe housing prices were going to start going down sooner rather than later."

The other fact Bass discovered in the early days of his research was that when it came to the mortgage market, there was no sheriff in town. "How many trillion-dollar markets that directly touch the consumer are you aware of that are unregulated?" Bass asks. The answer was that there was only one: the U.S. mortgage market. "This was a marketplace literally left to its own devices because there wasn't a regulator."

As 2006 progressed, Bass would discover what happens when a market is left to its own devices. In the late 1990s, he had done research on some of the problems then plaguing the tiny subprime lending industry and the companies in it (discussed in Chapter 2). He now revisited that industry and found that while most of the old firms were gone, a host of new ones with some of the same managers had replaced them. People's Choice Home Loan was one that he followed. "The guy that ran People's Choice had run Aames (Financial) into the ground and a few months after Aames's bankruptcy he founded People's Choice," Bass told me.

The same instincts that had led Bass to uncover frauds in the 1990s led him to take a closer look at Fremont General, one of the bigger providers of subprime loans. "The management team at Fremont was the same management team that went from zero in the workmans' comp insurance business to number two in the country in two-and-a-half years. Do you know why? They weren't reserving anything for the policies they were underwriting. The California Insurance Commission went in and closed their business and yet these same guys were running this institution that all of a sudden became one of the biggest subprime lenders in the country," explained Bass.

The deeper Bass looked, the more he sensed that the standards applied by these subprime lenders and all lenders had fallen appreciably. But it was still nothing more than a hunch.

At first, based on that hunch, Bass's natural inclination was to play the game he understood—shorting stocks.

He started to study up on the home builders in the belief that if credit stopped flowing quite so freely, their business would begin to suffer. But that didn't feel like the proper route to go. The stock market was strong in early 2006 and there was lots of chatter that home builders might become the next stop for the then-voracious private equity firms. They were on a historic buying spree of their own, made possible by the same decrease in lending standards that Bass was exploring in the housing market. It wouldn't be fun to be short a home builder's stock when it received a takeover offer.

Better, Bass thought, to keep digging. He began to research the subprime, alt-A, and prime mortgage markets by visiting with different Wall Street firms that bought these mortgages and made them into securities. He spoke with the bankers who were doing the securitizations as well as those who sat on a mortgage trading desk and bought *whole loans* from their originators. A whole loan is exactly what it sounds like. It is the actual mortgage made to a borrower.

This was a heady time for the whole loan market. Wall Street firms were paying high prices to buy whole mortgages, which they were packaging up as quickly as possible into mortgage-backed securities. As long as those mortgages stayed current for 90 days, the originator (lender) didn't have to give the money back. It was during a meeting with the whole loan trading desk at one of the biggest Wall Street firms that Bass began to believe his instincts were right.

"I'd sit down in the room with the head of whole loan trading who would be a few years out of business school and I would say, 'So, when do you think whole loan pricing will really start to come down? Are you guys worried about the quality of these loans that you're buying?' " The trader answered Bass calmly: "No, we're not worried about the quality. We just package 'em up and sell 'em as fast as we can," recalled Bass.

Bass kept pressing. "What if the Chinese [big buyers of mortgage-backed securities] don't want to buy any more of this stuff? What if they get burned?" he asked the head trader. The trader answered with a comment that Bass says he'll never forget: "Capital is ubiquitous today. It is free flowing and it will never stop." That stopped Bass cold. "He used the word *never*," explains Bass. "When you use absolute words like that on Wall Street, it's doing yourself and everyone else a disservice."

Bass asked the trader whether he had been around in 1998 when the credit markets briefly froze up after the failure of the hedge fund Long Term Capital. He asked him whether he remembered any of the subprime lenders such as FIRSTPLUS Financial and Aames Financial, which filed bankruptcy in the late 1990s. "Were you around when those companies blew apart?" Bass asked. The trader answered: "No, I was in B-school." Bass took a good look around and noted the fact that he was the only guy in the room over the age of 30. "Well, this is part of the problem right here, right now," Bass explains. "Here's the head of whole loan trading for one of the five biggest brokerage firms in the world who was in business school the last time there was a financial crisis."

Bass had effectively sized up what he was dealing with. It might have been an anecdotal piece of data, but for Bass it was all he needed to hear and see. "I came back from New York, met with my friends and the people working at my fund, and said, 'This is why this housing bubble exists today.' "

Now, the time had come for him to figure out the best way to make his bet that homes and the mortgages that financed their purchase were about to collapse in value. He knew he didn't want to simply short home builders, but what else could he do?

Bass had seen first-hand the abandon with which Wall Street trading desks were buying mortgages to package into securities. He knew what a subprime residential mortgage–backed security was, although he had yet to fully understand how it was constructed. He wondered if there was a way to effectively *short* a residential mortgage-backed security, and, if there was, Bass wondered whether it would be possible to find one made up of mortgages that were extended by the lenders with the lowest standards. Another journey into an opaque market filled with exotic structured products had begun.

Bass began a self-study course in securitization, reading and then rereading *Collateralized Debt Obligations: Structures and Analysis* by Laurie Goodman and Frank Fabozzi (Hoboken: John Wiley & Sons, 2002). He also started examining the pools of mortgages that made up a securitization, looking for the loans with consistently late payments or no payments at all and trying to follow them back to the lender that had originated them. Investors could do that if they chose to. The data was all there, but it was a time-consuming and complex process that almost all investors chose not to bother with. After all, these securities were often rated triple-A, so why bother to do any research? Bass's digging, however, would prove fruitful.

Bass ended up focusing on the home loans made by a medium-sized firm out of Irvine, California, run by a guy who wanted to be a film producer. He had found Daniel Sadek and Quick Loan Funding. "It was a reverse inquiry that got me there. I had never heard of him until I noticed how many of the loans that were coming out of that firm were not performing well," explains Bass.

Bass decided to put a call in to Quick Loan:

I mentioned I was a mortgage participant and very interested in their underwriting policies and procedures and how things were going. And this person on the phone went through why the firm exists and that they'll make a loan to anyone for anything as long as they can sell it and that it funded the budding film career of a guy named Sadek. I didn't make a judgment on Sadek. I just thought it all sounded kind of interesting.

Then Bass watched *Redline*, Sadek's movie:

They catapult two five-hundred-thousand-dollar cars and crash them and you find that Sadek let an actor drive his million-dollar

Ferrari into a wall. It was definitely worth looking into and the more you dig, the more you find.

Kyle recalls that Quick Loan had told him it would soon have a web site that would track the performance of its mortgages. "And I kept calling them to find out, because every time you pulled up the site, it would say 'This site is under construction.'" Bass called for months, asking when the site would go live. It never did.

"I don't mean to point at just one guy, because there were plenty of other firms with similar deficiencies," says Bass.

There was no real rhyme or reason to being a mortgage lender. You could just set up shop on the corner and make the most ridiculous loans you could make and as long as you could sell them and whoever you lent money to could make their payment for three months, you had no liability.

Bass had spent months researching the housing market of the United States. He was more certain than ever of his initial presumption. It *was* all going to end badly—*very* badly. Now, all Bass needed was to finally figure out his trade.

Bass had a friend named Alan Fournier who also ran a hedge fund (Penant Capital) and had been studying the same trends. Fournier had introduced Bass to the world of mortgage securitization and now that introduction would pay off. After his crash course in CDOs and securitization and some long talks with Fournier, Bass found the perfect way to profit from his belief that the house of cards built by homeowners, mortgage lenders, Wall Street bankers, and their regulators would soon come crashing down. It was in the synthetic CDO market.

As we learned in Chapter 7, the structured-products groups at banks weren't satisfied to simply pump out CDOs based on physical mortgage-backed securities. They needed to create a CDO made up of synthesized mortgages to keep feeding the demand for products.

In order to create those synthetic mortgages, the banks would sell credit protection, a form of insurance, on residential mortgage-backed securities. If the security in question went bad, the person holding the insurance would get paid off. If the security remained solvent, the buyer of the insurance was obligated to keep paying interest on the security for as long as he held the insurance (figure around 5 percent per year). That credit protection, known as a *credit default swap* (see Chapter 7), could be bundled together with other similar credit default swaps and sliced into different sections to create a synthetic CDO. The swap would also move up or down in value depending on the perceived likelihood that what it was insuring would default.

The banks *wanted* Bass to buy credit protection on their mortgage-backed securities because in doing so he gave them the opportunity to create synthetic CDOs that they could then get a big fee for selling. They also foolishly believed that their mortgages would never go bad. It took Bass months to wrap his head around the idea of a synthetic CDO.

"I would wonder why anybody would put together a synthetic obligation when there was a $12 trillion market of real mortgages in the United States. Why would you need more than that? Well, the answer was for more fees. Dealers get paid fees to structure synthetic CDOs." And with insatiable demand still coming from China, Asia, the Middle East, and Europe for dollar-denominated debt, the banks were happy to oblige these customers by creating synthetic CDOs.

This was a bet Bass couldn't pass up:

> In the cash marketplace, there's a real mortgage loan that's originated, pooled, packaged and sold as a cash bond to someone. It's not a zero-sum game. The synthetic market, on the other hand, is a zero-sum game. There is a winner. There is a loser. There is a seller and a buyer and they just agree to look at a reference obligation and pay each other based on what that obligation does.

The *reference obligation* in this case was the layer of a mortgage-backed security at the bottom of the stack—the one that would be swamped if as little as 3 percent of the mortgages in the pool defaulted.

It was the greatest trade Bass had ever encountered. Not just because he felt so certain his research on the mortgage market would prove correct, but because the trade had little downside even if it went against him:

I could hardly believe what I was seeing. Because with an equity [stock], you can bet against an equity [short it] and have it double on you overnight. If you bet against a bond at par you have very small downside and very large upside if you think that bond will be impaired.

And Bass knew these bonds better than the banks that had put them together. His due diligence was far greater than any undertaken by the bank that had been buying these mortgages to stuff into mortgage-backed securities. He knew that within the BBB tranche of these mortgage-backed securities were mortgages originated by Daniel Sadek's Quick Loan Funding and other lenders with the same low standards—the mortgages that were sure to go bad the minute people could no longer refinance.

Bass also did something few other investors ever bothered to do. He read the prospectuses of the subprime mortgage-backed securities he was betting against. What he found only made him more certain. The mortgage-backed securities were supposed to contain what are known as *first-lien* mortgages. That means that if the borrower doesn't pay, the lender has the right to take the house and sell it and receive whatever proceeds are delivered from that sale. But when Bass read these prospectuses, he found that as much as 10 percent of the pool of mortgages were *second-lien* mortgages. "A second-lien loan is prioritized behind the first lien. So, when you read these prospectuses, buried deep within them you could find how many second-lien loans were in there," Bass explained.

Remember Arturo Trevilla? He had taken out two mortgages to buy his $584,000 home. One was a first-lien mortgage for the home, and the other mortgage, which financed Trevilla's down payment, had the second lien on the home. "In an environment where there was any stress on home prices," explains Bass, "we had the opinion that the second-lien mortgages on a home were worthless." After all, Arturo Trevilla was a subprime borrower who had put no money down to buy his home. If home prices went down, it was more than likely that the price the home would fetch in a foreclosure sale would relegate the second-lien mortgage to little if any recovery. All Bass needed was for

3 percent of the mortgages in a mortgage-backed security to go bad, and here he was finding that with any decrease in home prices it would probably be far worse than that.

The Investment of a Lifetime

In July 2006, after six months of research, Bass started feverishly putting his trades on. His main worry was that the collapse he foresaw would come too soon for him to place his bets. But as 2006 had moved along, nary a word was heard in the financial markets about the risk of a housing meltdown. Bass, ever the good short seller, kept doing his research. Before and after he put on his trades he kept finding the very people who would suffer the most if he was right and challenging them to tell him why he was wrong. In Bass's words:

> I guess I wanted to hear everybody's answer, anyone from a position of authority. I felt like I needed to bounce this off of everyone I could think of because given my opinion as to exactly what was going to transpire, it was going be an awful outcome.

His first stop was Bear Stearns. Bass had worked at Bear from 1994 until 2001 and was, at 28, one of the youngest senior managing directors in the firm's history. It was only a couple of days before he would begin investing hundreds of millions of dollars in hopes of profiting from the egregious mistakes he believed firms such as Bear had made. Bass's money came not only from his hedge fund but from a separate $110 million fund called the Subprime Credit Strategies Fund that he and a partner, Mark Hart of Corriente Advisors, had raised solely for the purpose of betting against the U.S. housing market.

Bass flew up to New York for a one-on-one meeting with Bear Stearns's chief risk officer, a meeting that had been arranged by a prospective investor in Bass's fund. As he walked into a conference room at Bear Stearns's towering headquarters in Midtown Manhattan, Bass was shocked to see a large group of people seated around a table awaiting his entrance. The chief risk manager was there, and he was joined

Kyle Bass (left) with Mark Hart of Corriente Advisors
Photo courtesy of Kyle Bass.

by Bear's head of Fixed Income Trading, the head of Mortgage Risk, and the executive who ran risk management for fixed income. These were the people entrusted with safeguarding the capital provided to Bear Stearns by its shareholders. They had all been deeply involved in the U.S. mortgage business for many years. Bear Stearns had built a hugely profitable business buying and securitizing mortgages and selling structured products such as CDOs made from mortgages. And now a guy from Dallas with a Texas twang and prophecies of Armageddon was here to tell them they had no idea what they had got themselves into.

Bass had brought along the 31-page presentation he and Mark Hart had used when raising money for their Subprime Credit Strategies Fund. It was filled with many of the facts Bass could recite from memory, such as the exponential growth in the issuance of subprime mortgages, the growing disparity between income and home prices, and the growing inventory of unsold homes. "Here I am, in this executive conference room filled with people very knowledgeable about this subject. And I was still a neophyte in their business. But in the end, that was a blessing," says Bass, "because people in this business had been brainwashed to think that home prices could never go down and they were very myopic about a few facts that were as clear as day to an outsider."

It was the summer of 2006. The Federal Funds rate was at 5.25 percent, its highest level since early 2001. Alan Greenspan and his replacement as Fed chairman, Ben Bernanke (who took over in early 2006), had raised interest rates 17 times since June 2004 in order to keep a lid on inflation.

A year later, the first rumblings of the credit crisis would begin at this very firm. But on that summer's day, the men who ran Bear Stearns and monitored its risk were not worried by the picture being painted by their former colleague. Bear Stearns's assets were equal to more than 38 times its equity. If those assets declined in value by only 3 percent, Bear's equity would be wiped out. It was a point Bass rested on when he came to the end of his presentation. "You realize if I'm right what's going to happen to you?" Bass asked. "How are you going to manage your risk as a firm?" He was quickly cut off by his host, Bear's chief risk officer. "You worry about your risk management and we'll worry about ours." As Bass was leaving the room, the same man put his arm around him as they walked out and whispered into his ear: "That's a very compelling presentation you've got there. God, I hope you're wrong."

Bass didn't stop there. He made his presentation to a prospective investor, who was clearly shaken by the weight of the thesis. The man was friendly with a governor of the Federal Reserve Board and insisted Bass do him the favor of discussing his views with people at the Federal Reserve. Bass obliged by making the trip to Washington, D.C., for what was a 40-minute meeting.

Bass gave a Fed official his view of the world. The response: "Jobs are still growing and incomes are still growing; we don't see it the same way."

"I understand," explains Bass. "I mean, they're thinking, 'Who is this guy from Dallas telling me what's about to happen with our world?'" The belief that home prices would remain stable as long as jobs were still being created and incomes were growing was a view widely shared by most economists and investors. But that view missed the key fact that the long historical relationship between median income and housing prices had gone far out of whack. "It's one of the reasons why Wall Street didn't understand how housing prices could fall abruptly," says Bass.

Bass wanted to understand the methodology by which the rating agencies stamped many of the securities he believed were junk with their highest investment-grade rating of triple-A. So he met with a housing analyst at Moody's and was shocked to discover that they, too, were firm believers that home prices would never decline. In fact, the analyst told Bass that their models called for an increase of between 6 and 8 percent in home prices for years to come.

As 2006 came to an end, Bass was anxiously monitoring anything and everything for signs the housing boom was over. It was still not clear he was going to be correct, so he decided to start 2007 with a visit to an unlikely place: the American Securitization Forum. This annual convention, held in Las Vegas, was mecca for all sellers and buyers of securitized products—chief among them, mortgages. The creators of this vast marketplace convened at the Venetian Hotel for their festive conclave.

Bass recalls one particular panel held in front of an audience of as many as 6,000 eager securitizers and their customers. On the panel was a man named John Devaney, a hedge fund manager who had made a fortune buying and selling securities backed by mortgages. "And he got up there and said, 'I don't care if loans go up or down in value or if homes go up or down in value. I make money in all markets.'" It was another one of those absolute comments that made Bass wince. At the time, the 37-year-old Devaney owned mansions in Key Biscayne and Aspen, a private jet, and a 150-foot yacht with the name *Positive Carry*. He would lose them all within 18 months.

As usual, Bass gained sustenance from his meetings with the "enemy"—the legions who believed housing prices were never coming down. He was relieved to find that there wasn't some secret they were all keeping from him that kept them confident. They simply chose to believe that the largest asset class in the United States was immune to cycles. It was while he was killing time at the bar of the Bellagio Hotel that Bass stumbled on the kind of evidence that made him almost certain 2007 would be his year. He was awaiting a dinner meeting with a group of mortgage company executives and struck up a conversation with the bartender.

I asked him how he was doin', and he said, "I'm not doin' so good," and I said, "Why not?" and he told me, "My three houses are killing me," and I said, "What do you mean, three houses?" He says, "You know I've been able to borrow and buy and flip some homes here in Vegas, so, you know, I own three of them now and I'm tryin' to rent two of them out 'cause I can't sell 'em."

Las Vegas was one of the epicenters of the housing boom in the United States. And here was a bartender at the Bellagio who had done what so many others in that neck of the woods had been doing for years: loading up on homes and the debt that came with them with the expectation that they could keep selling them for more than they paid.

As Bass's hedge fund reached the end of its first year of operation, he penned a letter to his investors. Since its inception in February 2006, Hayman Capital had gained 41 percent for those investors. It was a good year. But the gains had not come from Bass's big trade on the housing market. That was the trade Bass expected would now play out in the year ahead, and he detailed his thinking in his one-year investor letter.

Bass's letter overflows with all the facts he'd learned in 2006. It seems as though he can barely contain himself with his liberal use of capital letters and exclamation points as he tries to fit five years of financial history into a few paragraphs and scream of the pain he foresees for the world's financial system. To the uninitiated, little of it would make any sense with all those crazy acronyms and complex financial concepts and a writing style lacking in artistry. But in retrospect, coming as it did in January 2007, it is a work of brilliance and a roadmap for the future:

> We have purchased default protection on the lowest Moody's rated bonds (BBB flat and BBB–) of several subprime asset backed securities (ABS) through the credit default swap (CDS) market. Subprime lenders have allowed their underwriting policies to slip (or expire) as the largest housing bull market in history has carried on. We are now in a period of time that will redefine underwriting standards (or the lack thereof) of subprime lenders, the buying practices of whole loan buyers, the securitization

of subprime loans, and the unbridled issuance of Collateralized
Debt Obligations (CDOs) based on subprime RMBS.

In 1991, subprime issuance was below $20B. In 2006, subprime
originations totaled just over $600B. These loans have not been
tested in a period of time that is experiencing Home Price
Depreciation (HPD). The collective participants in the leveraged finance market have been unable to see the forest through
the trees. We are facing a 6 standard deviation event currently
with the housing affordability and income gap the widest it has
ever been. "Affordability" mortgage products that have been
dreamt up in recent years by the mortgage machine that Wall
Street has built in an effort to keep turning out product in the
face of 17 rate hikes from the Fed from June 2004 to today.

How many TRILLION DOLLAR markets that DIRECTLY
touch the consumer are you aware of that are UNREGULATED?
I don't know of one other than residential mortgage origination.
"Affordability" mortgage products are only effective as long as
there are additional "affordability" mortgage products available in
the future.

The last housing cycle downturn did not have a large subprime
component to its outstanding loans. The financing market was
also largely not distancing itself from the risk like it is today.
Back then, most originators were banks that held the loans as
investments and underwriting standards were more important. Today, there is an originator, a securitizor, and an ultimate
buyer of the securitized bonds. The risk of ownership of these
loans is transferred three times in less than 8 months!

In an environment of rapid Home Price Appreciation (HPA),
it became easy to refinance out of the problems and give
the borrower the ability to save his monthly cash flow from
destruction by using his home as the proverbial ATM machine.
The cost of the loan, pre-payment penalties and closing costs

were all simply rolled into the re-financed loan as home prices appreciated. In today's market HPD is trapping these equity-less borrowers in their current loans and will increase losses to these Asset Backed Securities (ABS) portfolios.

I have met with many of the top mortgage strategists and none have a clue as to what cumulative losses will be in a declining home price environment. IT SIMPLY HAS NEVER HAPPENED.

It was about to.

Chapter 11

And Then the Roof Caved In

"I don't believe that number," said Alan Greenspan. It was late 2005, and a staff member had just handed the Fed chairman a statistic he was sure was a mistake. "Who's published that number?" asked Greenspan. "The sample must be wrong."

The number in question detailed the percentage of mortgages that had been made in the United States that year that were subprime in classification. The number was 20 percent. "We knew that it was rising. But the whole [mortgage] market was essentially rising," Greenspan told me when we met face-to-face in September 2008. He still sounded incredulous. "That it would be 20 percent of originations? It maybe got up to 11? Maybe. But 20?"

The numbers Greenspan had been shown that day were true. One in every five mortgages made in the United States was a subprime mortgage. For Greenspan, it was a huge revelation. "Everybody in retrospect now knows that the boom was developing under the markets for quite a period of time, but nobody knew it then," contends the former Fed chairman. "In 2004, there was just no credible information on that. It wasn't until we got well into 2005 that the first inkling that [it] was developing was emerging."

It seems hard to believe. It's not as if there weren't countless anecdotes about home flippers in California and Florida and people who refinanced their mortgages once a year like clockwork, or that news of a housing boom wasn't featured on the covers of countless magazines, in newspapers, and on CNBC. Greenspan dismisses those stories, asserting that they are not indicative of the true state of affairs. "One of the things that you become very careful about if you're a supervisor or a regulator is to be careful of anecdotal evidence as a generic type of indication," counsels Greenspan. "We have a vast country. The amount of economic activity that goes on is truly awesome. We're dealing with hundreds of billions and trillions of dollars. And it is remarkable how big certain small things look."

The data, says Greenspan, is what matters. And while it may be easy for people to look back now and say it was all so obvious, the man who ran the Federal Reserve during the greatest decline in lending standards our nation has ever seen is not willing to admit he missed it:

> You say, "Well, why wasn't it obvious?" Well, the problem is, supposing you have twenty such "anecdotal" things going on. You remember the one that worked and forget the other nineteen. It's a classic problem of supervision and regulation. What people don't realize is the reason regulators sometimes don't move on certain things is not that they don't perceive it to be a potential problem. But they've also had the experience that nine out of ten such problems disappear on their own.

Clutching that report in late 2005, Greenspan, perhaps for the first time, was coming to grips with the fact that the problem of subprime mortgages was not going to disappear on its own. And as he dug in more deeply, Greenspan realized the reason it wasn't going to go away. "The subprime market went from seven percent of total originations to twenty percent in three years . . . because it became securitized in a vast way and internationally," explains Greenspan. "Certainly in retrospect that had a wholly unforeseen effect."

The Wheels Coming Off

In 2006, housing prices stopped going up and lending standards stopped going down. The two, of course, were closely linked. It wasn't clear at first. These things are tough to see immediately. Bill Dallas may have been one of the first to spot the coming storm as he tried to steer the mortgage lender he ran, Ownit, to calmer waters. Dallas tightened the company's lending standards in hopes of surviving what he believed would be a nasty downturn. By the middle of 2006, Ownit had reduced its monthly production of new mortgages from $1 billion a month to about $600 million, given it was approving far fewer mortgages.

Dallas had made it tougher for people to get a mortgage, but it didn't stop the lesser-quality mortgages Ownit had already doled out from coming back to haunt it. Delinquencies were increasing by the day. "When we started to peel back the onion, you could see that all the things that we worried about were coming to bear," recalls Dallas. Mortgages given to people with low credit scores whose incomes had not been verified were going bad fast. Dallas decided at the end of 2006 to shut Ownit down rather than meet a big margin call from Merrill Lynch. His was one of the first mortgage lenders in the country to go out of business. It would be far from the last.

The Wall Street firms that were buying mortgages from firms like Ownit also started to see signs of impending doom as 2006 came to a close. Banker Michael Francis explains:

> The first red flag is that your delinquencies in general start to go up at thirty, sixty, and ninety days. They were usually one percent [of the securitization pool], maybe two percent, but now they were two percentage points higher than that.

Firms like Francis's that assembled the mortgages and securitized them were at the end of the chain in the origination process. By the time Francis and his team were sending mortgage-backed securities out to the world, the mortgages they were created from had been around for four or five months. In more typical times, that was not a problem. But when you're at the end of the biggest downturn in lending standards the housing market has ever seen and housing prices have stopped going up, things go bad pretty quickly. "We would put those loans into our deal and within sixty days of the security being sold, the delinquencies would rapidly be approaching the six, seven, eight, or nine percent range very, very quickly," recalls Francis.

When 9 percent of the mortgages from a securitization are being paid late or not at all, it's a very bad sign. "The wheels were starting to come off," says Francis. Wall Street's mortgage machine was sputtering as the links in the mortgage chain began to be pulled apart.

The forces behind that pull were apparent to people like Bill Dallas and Michael Francis. Mortgage brokers had long ago run out of people with good credit to sell mortgages to and now they were running out of people with bad credit to sell mortgages to. Some Wall Street firms began to pull back from the mortgage business, which meant it was that much tougher for mortgage originators to find the cash they needed to extend new home loans. Such was the case for Ownit, which, after trying to navigate a difficult market by tightening its lending standards, chose to give up and close down. The end result: There was less credit available for would-be homeowners.

The great ocean of credit that had fueled the housing boom started to dry up. Credit, it turned out, was not ubiquitous. And when it started going away, getting a home loan for those who couldn't qualify for a traditional fixed-rate, prime mortgage became more expensive. That kept new buyers from being able to afford a home.

If this had been any other period in the history of the U.S. housing market, the disappearance of these previously "marginal" buyers would not have had a great impact on the vast market for homes in the United States. But this was the housing market of 2006, in which over 40 percent of all new mortgages (subprime and Alt-A) were made to non-prime borrowers. The marginal buyer had become a major player, and when these buyers could no longer get a home loan, the impact was sizable. Home prices stopped rising.

Rising prices had been the elixir that everyone connected with the business of residential mortgages relied on to keep the machine running. When home prices were rising, the freedom to refinance was manna from heaven. You could refinance to pay off your credit card bills or put in a new pool. You could refinance in hopes of using your newfound equity to start a business, as Arturo Trevilla hoped to do. But most important, the freedom to refinance allowed people to escape exotic mortgage products before they became toxic. There was no concern about the higher rate that was coming if the buyer knew she could simply step into yet another mortgage that would delay those higher payments for two or three more years.

When home prices stopped rising, the freedom to refinance got taken away. People with mortgages they could not afford suddenly found themselves without an exit strategy. And so they began to stop paying their mortgages back.

The Call

It was February 2007. I hadn't been talking to money manager Kyle Bass as regularly as I used to. He'd been busy launching his hedge fund and both our days of chasing down frauds seemed to be over. The few times we had spoken, Bass had shown a surprisingly strong interest in broad investment themes like the price of oil and the price of homes. He once asked me to track down a report that appeared on the *NBC Nightly News* about rising home values. I couldn't imagine why it was of so much interest to him.

The call was like a lightning bolt. "David," said the Texas twang on the other end of the phone. "Do you realize what is happening?"

"Kyle? Is that you?"

"David, do—you—realize—what—is—happening?"

Obviously, I was not at all sure of what was happening, but it seemed pretty certain that I was about to find out.

I still have my notes from the call. The page is filled with words and phrases that I was hearing for the first time: *CDOs; $100 billion in subprime mezzanine tranches; ABX Index; 1100 is mid-06-BBB on the index; '06 CDO issuance—$200 billion.* And there were some things that I understood pretty well: *Mortgage market imploding; Someone is losing a lot of $; Merrill has the most exposure to CDOs; Bear is in trouble; It's very bad; Can't ramp the warehousing line.*

In the months to come, I would slowly begin to make sense of the avalanche of information Bass unleashed on that February afternoon. The reason for his call was due to the release of so-called *remittance data* earlier that day. If you own a piece of a mortgage securitization, you receive data on the 25th of each month telling you how many of the mortgages in the securitization pool are 30 days delinquent, 60 days delinquent, 90 days delinquent, or in default.

On February 25, 2007, the remittance data was bad. It showed a sudden spike in delinquencies. It was a spike that Kyle had been expecting for months, but it caught most investors off guard. "All of Wall Street said, 'Wait a minute, these loan delinquencies are not supposed to spike like this,'" Bass said. An index that had been created to track the value of the BBB and BBB– pieces of mortgage securitizations fell sharply in value. Kyle's credit protection on those same securities rose sharply in value. He was about to become a very wealthy man.

Delinquencies did not trend much higher in March 2007 and the uneventful data from the spring months, when people were likely getting tax refunds that helped them pay their mortgages, convinced many that February had been an aberration. The index that tracked the various slices of mortgage securitizations rebounded sharply from February. People were breathing a sigh of relief.

But not the people who ran the largest subprime lenders in the nation. They were done. In March 2007, in rapid succession, Fremont General, New Century, People's Choice, and Ameriquest announced they were closing their lending operations. The funding these firms had relied on from Wall Street was drying up.

In 2006, New Century had made roughly $60 billion worth of subprime loans. Now, facing mounting defaults on those same loans, the banks that gave it funding pulled away. In the good times, New Century sold its mortgages to Morgan Stanley, Goldman Sachs, Barclays, Citigroup, Credit Suisse, and other Wall Street firms, and they in turn provided the credit lines that kept its origination machine humming. But that February's remittance data was scaring away the investors who used to buy the mortgage-backed securities these firms sold, and so *they* were now pulling back as well. Michael Francis would soon lose his job on Wall Street. He now runs ExMor Capital, a firm that counsels mortgage lenders.

New Century, Fremont, and Ameriquest were among the top-10 subprime lenders in the nation in 2006. By March 2007, they were out of the business. Soon they would all collapse. Over the ensuing months, more than 40,000 people who worked in the subprime industry would lose their jobs, including Lou Pacific from Quick Loan Funding.

Quick Loan, which at its height employed 700 people and had handed out about $4 billion worth of subprime loans, somehow managed to hang on until the summer of 2007, when it, too, was forced to close its doors. Today, its founder, Daniel Sadek, is broke. He told me so himself. After refusing numerous requests for an interview for more than a year, Sadek called me at my CNBC office in February 2009 to tell me that Quick Loan was far from the worst offender when it came to subprime mortgages. "We didn't do loans where you weren't allowed to make a pre-payment and we would agree to reduce people's interest rates," said Sadek.

Sadek knows about that kind of forbearance. After he fell two months behind in his mortgage payments to Citigroup, the bank's Residential Lending unit offered to modify its loan terms so he could meet his mortgage payments. Sadek, according to the reporting of John Gittelsohn of the *Orange County Register*, did not make a single payment after the loan modification. Citigroup subsequently issued him a notice of default and is in the process of foreclosing on his home.

A Crisis Begins

It's always nice to date things: July 4, 1776 (U.S. independence); November 11, 1918 (end of World War I); June 6, 1944 (invasion of Normandy). You get the idea. Somehow, it's comforting to know when important events began and when they ended. So I understand the desire to date the beginning of the crisis in the world's credit markets that gave rise to the largest economic crisis our nation has seen since the Great Depression. But as with the Great Depression (which some date to the stock market crash of October 29, 1929 and others say did not begin until later), it's not easy to say when the global credit crisis truly began.

One might argue that the credit crisis began on June 20, 2007, when two highly leveraged hedge funds run by Bear Stearns found themselves near collapse. The funds were heavily invested in CDOs, and, because of the recent drop in value of those securities, they were in danger of getting those CDOs sold out from under them by the investment banks that lent the hedge funds money.

It was one of those occasions that warranted a call from Kyle Bass. I had been a poor student. Despite his erratic efforts to educate me on the structure of CDOs and the subprime securitization market, I had not advanced far from our first conversation on this subject in February. On this day, I was to learn of still-more-esoteric CDO-related products, such as *CDO-squareds* (A CDO made up of other CDOs), and was quickly informed that the prices of all CDOs based on subprime mortgages were not worth anywhere near what their owners were saying they were worth. Bass's hedge fund and the fund he raised to bet exclusively against the mortgage market were soaring in value. His investments would ultimately be up 600 percent over the 18 months he held them. The profits for his investors would total over $2 billion. It was a once-in-a-lifetime trade.

In late June 2007, Bear Stearns initially managed to stave off the collapse of its two hedge funds by infusing capital into the funds and convincing many of the banks that had lent the funds money to allow them to keep operating. A little more than a month later, with the market for all subprime-related securities falling still further, the hedge funds collapsed anyway. The Bear Stearns High-Grade Structured Credit Strategies Master Fund and the High-Grade Structured Credit Strategies Enhanced Leverage Master Fund filed for bankruptcy in the Cayman Islands and sought an orderly liquidation of assets. The bankruptcy did limited damage to Bear Stearns's stock price at the time, which hovered around $120 a share.

Alan Greenspan is unequivocal. He says the credit crisis began on August 9, 2007, when the French bank BNP Paribas suspended trading in three of its mutual funds. The funds had been large buyers of securities backed by U.S. subprime mortgages; unable to find willing buyers for those securities and therefore establish a value for them, BNP Paribas halted withdrawals from the funds. That event set off a panic in the short-term credit markets.

I prefer to date the start of the credit crisis to July 10, 2007. On that day, the credit rating agency Standard & Poor's announced that it would shortly downgrade its credit ratings on billions of dollars' worth of mortgage-backed securities comprised of subprime mortgages. Also likely, said S&P, was a wave of downgrades of CDOs made up of any of those mortgage-backed securities. And in a monumental admission that it had misjudged the creditworthiness of such mortgages (my words, not theirs), S&P said it was revising the way it went about judging just how likely subprime borrowers were to pay their mortgages back. And why did it do so?

Here are S&P's rationale and my translation of what the firm was actually saying:

> Loss rates, which are being fueled by shifting patterns in loss behavior and further evidence of lower underwriting stand-ards and misrepresentations in the mortgage market, remain in excess of historical precedents and our initial assumptions.

> *Translation:* We totally missed the fact that no lenders cared about whether people could pay back their mortgages and we've started to sense that some of these people "exaggerated" how much money they were earning.

> New data reveals that delinquencies and foreclosures continue to accumulate at an increasing rate for the 2006 vintage. We see poor performance of loans, early payment defaults, and increas-ing levels of delinquencies and losses.

> *Translation:* Wow, these loans made in 2006 are going bad fast!

> On a macroeconomic level, home prices will continue to come under stress. Weakness in the property markets contin-ues to exacerbate losses, with little prospect for improvement in the near term. Furthermore, we expect losses will continue to increase, as borrowers experience rising loan payments due to the resetting terms of their adjustable-rate loans and princi-pal amortization that occurs after the interest-only period ends for both adjustable-rate and fixed-rate loans.

Translation: Home prices are done going up and now these people with these ridiculous mortgages are screwed.

As lenders have tightened underwriting guidelines, fewer refinance options may be available to these borrowers, especially if their loan-to-value (LTV) and combined LTV (CLTV) ratios have risen in the wake of declining home prices.

Translation: You can't refinance a mortgage that's worth more than the home it is supporting. Did we tell you these people are screwed?

Data quality is fundamental to our rating analysis. The loan performance associated with the data to date has been anomalous in a way that calls into question the accuracy of some of the initial data provided to us regarding the loan and borrower characteristics.

Translation: Did we mention that we think there is fraud here? Sorry we missed it at first, but that's not our job.

Given all of these current factors, we are refining our surveillance approach for subprime RMBS transactions issued from the fourth quarter of 2005 through the fourth quarter of 2006. Going forward, the ratings methodology for new transactions will also incorporate these factors.

Translation: Now that it's too late, we're going to tell you what these mortgages are really worth.

In addition, we have modified our approach to reviewing the ratings on senior classes in a transaction in which subordinate classes have been downgraded. Historically, our practice has been to maintain a rating on any class that has passed our stress assumptions and has had at least the same level of outstanding credit enhancement as it had at issuance. Going forward, there will be a higher degree of correlation between the rating actions on classes located sequentially in the capital structure.

A class will have to demonstrate a higher level of relative protection to maintain its rating when the class immediately subordinate to it is being downgraded.

Translation: None of this stuff is going to be triple-A for much longer. Sorry about that.

The ignorant foreign buyers who had been voraciously feeding on anything with a triple-A rating suddenly realized they had been had. They had never read the fine print in a CDO or RMBS prospectus. They had looked only at the triple-A rating. They had relied on a corrupt system, little of which they understood. Now they understood one key truth. The reason triple-A credits never default isn't because the initial credit rating is accurate. It's because the rating agencies will always *downgrade* them before they default. Triple-A doesn't mean triple-A for life—not even close.

When that lesson was learned, the buyers Wall Street had counted on to keep devouring all those securities it concocted out of mortgages left the scene. No one wanted to buy this stuff anymore—not the banks in mainland China or the Chinese government, not the banks or insurance companies in Taiwan or Korea or Germany or France or the United Kingdom. They were done, and not just with products structured from mortgages. All those buyers with their "excess pools of liquidity" started to have a well-deserved crisis of confidence in any security that had previously been given a strong credit rating. After all, if the rating agencies did such a poor job of ascertaining the risk of subprime mortgage securities, why would anyone believe their failure was an isolated event?

And that was the start of the credit crisis.

The CDO Blues

It's a funny thing to compare Merrill Lynch's 2006 annual report with the same report from 2007. In the 2006 annual report, a search for the acronym *CDO* finds no matches. Not one mention of the product that would figure so prominently in its demise. A search in the 2007 annual report for the term *CDO* finds more than 100 matches.

Did Merrill's business really change that much in a year? Of course not. It was the same company doing the same things. But in 2007, Merrill had to start telling its investors about CDOs because it was losing so much money from them. In the second half of 2007, as the credit markets seized up and any security with a mortgage in it could no longer be sold, Merrill found itself in a tough position.

It had begun the year with all guns blazing as it sought to dominate the market for securitized mortgage products. It was not prepared in any way to deal with the devastating impact from the credit crisis. It takes months to put together a CDO, given its components. A firm needs to keep thousands of mortgages in-house to create mortgage-backed securities and then needs even more time to rejigger them to create CDOs. As well, many firms kept certain parts of the CDOs they could not sell in the belief they were money-good. Merrill had played a terrible game of musical chairs. It wasn't left standing when the music stopped. It was left in the fetal position.

The writedowns came swiftly and kept getting worse. By the end of 2007, Merrill Lynch had absorbed losses of $23.2 billion from its business of buying, packaging, and selling investment products made from subprime mortgages. The vast majority of those losses came specifically from CDOs made up of asset-backed securities. But the damage wasn't confined to those products. The absence of buyers for any fixed-income security led to a decline in the value of all fixed-income securities and there were plenty of those on the balance sheet of every financial company in the world.

Citigroup, Wachovia, Washington Mutual, UBS, Bank of America, Morgan Stanley, Lehman Brothers, Bear Stearns, Fannie Mae, and Freddie Mac were among the most notable financial companies that would end 2007 in a seriously weakened state thanks to their participation in the U.S. mortgage market. It wasn't just that those firms owned mortgages and mortgage-related securities. It was also what they had chosen to do with their balance sheets.

These public companies, in their race to enhance returns (the compensation of their senior executives was often linked to those returns), had mightily increased their use of leverage. Many of them had equity (the capital controlled by the institution) that was as little as 2 or 3 percent of the total amount of assets on their balance sheets. The way they financed those assets was by borrowing money from other financial institutions. That borrowed money is what is known as *leverage*. Leverage is like alcohol. It makes the good times better and the bad times worse. And times were about to get a whole lot worse.

Lights Out

Merrill Lynch ended 2007 with $1,020,050,000,000 worth of assets on its balance sheet. If you're wondering what that number is, given all the commas, it is a little over one trillion dollars. Merrill's tangible equity (equity capital less goodwill and other intangible assets) at the end of 2007 was $31.566 billion. The firm's assets (what was owed) represented roughly 32 times its equity capital (what it owned). A 3 percent drop in the value of Merrill's assets would wipe out its equity capital.

That's exactly what began to happen to Merrill Lynch. It ended 2007 with a pre-tax loss for the year of $12.8 billion (while it lost far more than that in the second half of the year, it had earned money during the first half) and would need to quickly replenish its equity capital. The firm, under the leadership of new CEO John Thain, raised roughly $13 billion during the last quarter of 2007 and the first quarter of 2008, through the issuance of common and preferred stock. It would prove to be far too little.

In 2008, Merrill Lynch would lose $41.19 billion before taxes. In 15 months it had managed to lose $54 billion, the vast majority of it coming as a result of Stan O'Neal's fateful decision to take more and more risk and plunge Merrill Lynch into the deep end of the mortgage securitization market. O'Neal is a very smart man. Anyone who knows him will tell you that. And one of his strongest suits is math. He understands numbers in the way few people can. Yet the risk management model at Merrill Lynch completely failed, as it did at financial giants such as Citigroup, Lehman Brothers, UBS, AIG, Bear Stearns, Fannie Mae, and so many others.

Former Federal Reserve Chairman Alan Greenspan says there is a reason those models failed so miserably. "The mathematics of it and the economics of it are very sophisticated." The trouble, says Greenspan, is that the formulas the banks used to extrapolate risk were based on data from a period of economic expansion. The banks used *periods of euphoria* rather than *periods of fear* on which to base their risk management decisions. "The coefficients that you will get in a period of fear would have told them that the degree of leverage they were taking was very risky," says Greenspan. "The problem was in the data, not in the mathematics."

Wherever the problem may have been, Greenspan believes the executives who ran our nation's large financial institutions ultimately *did* understand the risk they were taking. "I spoke to them," says Greenspan. In those conversations with the leaders of the financial system, Greenspan says he would remind them of how easy it had become to borrow money for even the riskiest of credits. Risk, says Greenspan, had become severely underpriced. He cites as an example, and one he shared with many CEOs, the fact that companies with an atrocious credit rating of CCC could borrow at only 4 percent more than the U.S. Treasury. In far different times, triple-C-rated companies would have to pay *24 percent* more than the U.S. Treasury for their money.

"It was extraordinary. Everyone was aware of it [the underpricing of risk]. But what they all recognized is if they didn't participate, or as Chuck Prince [former CEO of Citigroup] said, 'if they don't participate and dance on the floor, they will irretrievably lose market share,'" argues Greenspan.

> And that's precisely the issue. It wasn't that all of these people were caught by surprise. They were caught in a terrible dilemma that yes, they could protect their shareholders and they could be sitting there for years with a good balance sheet. But their status in the marketplace would be going down, down, down as would the value in their stock market capitalization.

Executives such as Chuck Prince (CEO, Citigroup), Jimmy Cayne (CEO, Bear Stearns), Dick Fuld (CEO, Lehman brothers), and Stan O'Neal had all been around for a long time. They had lived through the short-term crisis in the debt markets brought on by the collapse of the hedge fund Long Term Capital in October 1998. They had seen plenty of history and Greenspan submits that they knew exactly what they were doing. The problem, says the former Fed chief, is that they all thought they knew when to get out.

Greenspan may have been warning the CEOs to be careful, but he did little more than that. As their chief regulator, he believed they would make the right decisions to safeguard their institutions. It was a significant error. And whereas Alan Greenspan may have believed the CEOs all understood the risk they were taking, after speaking with people close to Stan O'Neal, it is clear to me that while he may have understood his firm was taking too much risk, he didn't fully appreciate the nature of that risk.

Up until the summer of 2007, insiders tell me O'Neal didn't ask many detailed questions about Merrill Lynch's mortgage business. He didn't ask, and given the culture he had created at the firm, there wasn't anyone who was going to volunteer even the idea that the business could run off the rails.

O'Neal had fired Jeff Kronthal, who oversaw much of Merrill Lynch's fixed-income business, in the summer of 2006, after Kronthal resisted attempts to take more risk and had the temerity to tell O'Neal that to his face. The people who inherited Kronthal's responsibilities weren't about to tell Stan O'Neal something he didn't want to hear, especially given how much money they were all making. It was not until late in the summer of 2007 that O'Neal started "digging in" to the mess he'd made of Merrill Lynch, according to people who worked closely with him.

Stan O'Neal ran a vast company with over 60,000 employees and tens of thousands of shareholders. I realize the hectic nature of our world and the myriad distractions that can keep an executive from focusing on one part of a large enterprise. But I still can't imagine how it is possible that Stan O'Neal wasn't "digging in" to fully understand the mortgage market of which his firm was such an important part, particularly because this was not a matter of experience or intelligence. Ask people who know Stan O'Neal to describe him and the two adjectives they come up with are *smart* and *mean*. Those two characteristics are usually a good combination for running a financial services company.

By the middle of August 2007, with the credit crisis underway, Stan O'Neal was dug in. Perhaps it came to him when he learned of the complexity of synthetic CDOs and started to appreciate the risk Merrill Lynch had taken on with that product. Or maybe he dug in on the credit side of the spectrum and came to grips with the fact that mortgages his firm had been buying were being given to people who couldn't pay them back. Whatever the curriculum in his studies, he finally knew the truth: Merrill Lynch was in deep trouble. He would probably lose his job. And the fact of his knowing this probably meant it was too late to alter either outcome.

Those lonely rounds of golf in the late summer of 2007 may have offered O'Neal the opportunity to focus on what he could do to try to save Merrill. And to his credit, insiders tell me he returned after Labor Day determined to sell the company to Bank of America. A deal may have been in hand for as much as $80 a share, but Merrill's board vetoed it.

O'Neal stepped down as Merrill's CEO on October 30, 2007. In the waning days of that month, all but certain that he would soon be asked to leave, O'Neal retreated to his executive suite. A senior manager recalls walking toward O'Neal's office to ask a question. He approached, but at seeing the room was dark, began to back away. Still, he gave the slightly ajar door a knock and was surprised to hear a reply from within. He entered. Stan O'Neal's lights were off. He was sitting in the dark. And as the visitor came closer, he heard O'Neal repeating something over and over.

"I should have known better . . . I should have known better. . . ."

Epilogue

The sun comes up. The kids wake up. And another day begins. I drive the 10 miles to CNBC headquarters and start my workday. Each morning, I do many of the same things I've been doing at CNBC for the past 16 years. I get in a bit later than I should. I make some calls to see what's going on and what situations might provide me an opportunity to do some additional reporting so I can share valuable insights with our viewers. I run down to the makeup room and allot them the three minutes until airtime to make me look presentable (it gets tougher with each passing year). I sit on the set for my show and proceed to make more phone calls and converse with my producer about whatever it is I've decided to talk about for my first appearance of the morning. And then I start to speak.

I might be reporting on the latest doings with a potential acquisition or I might be sharing some news on the state of our nation's banks or hedge funds or private equity firms. It is what I get paid to do and I still enjoy doing it. But somehow it doesn't feel quite right. While I might be reporting on the same type of events that have been taking place for years and the people responsible for creating those events have likewise been doing so for years, we are no longer doing it in the financial world that we grew up with. That world ended in September 2008 and we've been dealing with the consequences ever since.

On some occasions, I find myself suppressing a desire to stop my report and get up and start shouting at the camera, "Do you have any idea what has happened to our financial system? Do you realize it has been turned upside-down and inside-out and no one is quite sure of anything anymore?" Because it's true. The ground has been shifting beneath the financial world we once knew and no one is quite certain what the landscape will look like when it stops shifting.

Each day seems to bring new pronouncements about what U.S. financial institutions can and cannot do. At this very moment, scores of executives at our nation's banks are scouring the fine print in an economic stimulus bill that recently became law and are trying to determine how much money they can pay themselves each year. The U.S. government is keeping the financial system afloat through a series of support mechanisms the likes of which our financial markets have never seen, and so our elected officials seem to be in more control of these companies than their own leaders.

Amazingly, the United States is in a lot less trouble than much of the rest of the world. We are less exposed to the radical economic deterioration taking place than many of our trading partners, who are dealing with large budget deficits, failing banks, and a tax base too small to help bail them out.

Countries in Eastern Europe that feasted for years on cheap loans from banks in Western Europe now find themselves unable to pay back the money. Their economies—which were based on producing goods for the U.S. market—have collapsed.

Now there is a real fear that a cascade of sovereign defaults in Eastern Europe will overwhelm Western Europe's banks. And if those banks fail, can their governments bail them out in the same way the United States has saved its banks?

While it has tried to avoid "nationalizing" financial institutions, the U.S. government was forced to take ownership of three of the largest financial institutions in the world. AIG, Fannie Mae, and Freddie Mac seem likely to compete with each other for the title of the largest loss in financial history before this crisis ends. At present, AIG alone has cost the

U.S. taxpayer $162 billion. It has been the largest recipient by far of government money. All those credit default swaps it wrote with nary a care in the world have cost us all. It makes one wonder whether we might have been better off just letting it fail and dealing with the consequences since many of those same consequences seem to have been delivered anyway.

The U.S. government saved Citigroup from near-certain collapse by guaranteeing hundreds of billions of its loans to consumers and corporations, and that still wasn't enough to keep it propped up. Now, taxpayers own 36 percent of the once-mighty bank after coming to its rescue for a third time.

The largest single component of the loan portfolio the U.S. taxpayer is now standing behind for Citigroup is mortgage loans, about $154 billion of them. If you want a sign this crisis is far from over, you need look no further than Citigroup's decision to include all those mortgages in the pool of assets the government is guaranteeing. If Citigroup thought they were money-good, they wouldn't be there. A similar, though smaller (roughly $100 billion), guarantee has also been provided to Bank of America, another of the largest lending institutions in our country.

Lazard Freres is now the largest investment bank in the United States. That's because Morgan Stanley and Goldman Sachs, after watching their former competitors at Lehman Brothers and Bear Stearns collapse, ran to the shelter provided by the bank holding company structure. It's not clear what the new model for making money is at these companies, now that the old model—reliance on excessive amounts of leverage to generate rich returns—appears dead. As the recipient of billions in government money and under the now-strict supervision of the Federal Reserve, it's hard to imagine these companies will be allowed to take the kind of risk they did in the past.

These days, of course, none of them are interested in taking risk. They are most interested in avoiding it. After years of lending money to consumers and corporations with fewer and fewer strings attached, our banks are quickly backpedaling. Standards that might recently have seemed quaint are back in fashion.

The banks raised money furiously in 2008 until there were simply no private investors left to tap. That's a key problem these days. Banks cannot raise capital at almost any price. They can't even sell debt. As of this writing, the only unsecured debt sold for months in the entire banking sector that was not backed by the government has been a paltry $2 billion raised by Goldman Sachs.

With no one else to turn to, the banks have turned to the government. While more than $700 billion of our taxpayer money has been "lent" to financial institutions both large and small in an attempt to shore up their balance sheets, it is a simple fact that at this moment many of the most important financial institutions in this country, just like Citigroup, remain technically insolvent. If they were forced to sell their assets at current market prices, there is no way their tangible equity would be enough to withstand the massive losses they would suffer as a consequence of those sales.

They are dead men walking—hoping they can walk far enough to reach a point beyond the current crisis when profits will be restored along with their financial viability. It may be a long walk.

At present count, the world's banks have lost $1.2 trillion since the credit crisis began in the summer of 2007. Most of those losses are directly related to the collapse of the mortgage market in the United States. The rest came as a result of the crisis brought on by that collapse. One might hope that more than a trillion dollars' worth of losses would be enough—that it would represent the necessary writedowns on all the mortgages and mortgage-backed securities made from those mortgages and CDOs constructed from those mortgage-backed securities and credit default swaps written to provide insurance on those mortgage-backed securities and CDOs. But it won't be.

The decline in lending standards detailed in the pages of this book may be neatly summarized as the *subprime problem*. But as you have read, it was not confined to that subset of the mortgage market. While notices of defaults (which are sent after a homeowner misses three or four payments) have subsided for subprime loans, they have started to surge in the rest of the mortgage market. That's because during the boom many prime borrowers were not really prime.

Who better to explain than Kyle Bass:

Imagine you're a subprime borrower in 2004 and you refinanced your loan in 2005 into a bigger loan so you could cash out some money. So if you cash out and refinance, your credit score goes up because you just paid off a huge loan. So your first loan might have been subprime, but on your next loan you're a prime borrower.

In a market where housing prices rose, those borrowers might still be considered prime. But with prices down they are nothing more than a subprime tenant in a house that's worth less than their mortgage.

While subprime mortgage debt totals about $1.2 trillion and alt-A mortgages around $1.5 trillion, the prime mortgage market totals $10 trillion. Even small percentage losses in that market add up to huge numbers. And they are coming.

Jumbo prime mortgages, which are mortgages above the amount that Fannie and Freddie will buy, have seen a surge in delinquencies. Securitizations comprised of these mortgages are seeing delinquency rates above 7 percent. And delinquencies among prime borrowers whose mortgages are eligible for sale to Fannie and Freddie are also surging.

The rating agencies, after owning up to the error of their ways in July 2007, have been assaulting every known securitization made up of mortgages ever since. In the summer of 2008, S&P yet again revised its loss assumptions on every type of mortgage securitization. The other rating agencies have done the same, taking securities they once rated triple-A to levels that make them the junk they always were.

It may get worse before it gets better, because housing prices are still falling. The economic forecasting team at Goldman Sachs recently did a study of housing busts in countries that belong to the Organization for Economic Cooperation and Development. They studied 24 so-called housing busts that have taken place since the 1970s. Each saw at least a 15 percent decline in real home prices (after inflation) with the average decline over 30 percent. Kyle Bass believes we are only two years into a six-year bottoming process in which prices will fall an average of 35 percent nationwide from peak to trough.

The banks may have already written off $1.2 trillion, but economists at the International Monetary Fund believe we have at least another trillion dollars' worth of writedowns to come. It's not just mortgages and mortgage-related products any longer. With a brutal recession in full swing, loans of all types to consumers and businesses are bound to suffer. When one thinks of a company such as Bank of America with $690 billion in consumer-related loans and commercial loans of $337 billion, it's easy to understand why it may be on the dole for a while longer.

I recently ran into Meg Whitman, the former CEO of eBay, who is running for governor of California. Meg is a first-class lady—smart, focused, and decent. Why in the world she wants to run the state of California is beyond me. Meg told me that in the Inland Empire of California, one in every four homes is in foreclosure. Many of the homes built in those former cow pastures now sit empty, their lawns no longer cared for and a No Trespassing sign pasted to the front window.

Joe and Barbara Dunkley, who bought early in the boom and sold at its peak, were among the lucky ones. They made a profit of $250,000 on a house they had paid $300,000 for only a couple of years earlier. But the Dunkleys decided to stay in the Inland Empire and rent a home. Sure enough, the home they rented was foreclosed on. It seems that even the lucky ones haven't been able to escape.

Back on Wall Street, there has also been no escape. Tens of thousands of people have lost their jobs at the banks that helped create the economic crisis and each day more jobs are cut. The collateral damage has been even greater. Americans watched their retirement savings vanish as the equity markets plummeted in 2008 and early 2009, while their net worth also declined due to the precipitous fall in home values.

There was nowhere to hide. Not in stocks or bonds or hedge funds or private equity. Although there have been a handful of stars such as Kyle Bass, the vast multitude of professional investors got it wrong.

And yet there is still a hope on Wall Street that while things will be different for a period of time, they won't change for all time. And when I talk about *change*, I am referring specifically to *compensation*— the compensation of the people who work at the banks that fueled the mortgage madness that consumed the world's economy; the compensation of the private equity bankers who thrived on the cheap-and-plentiful debt they could use to buy up enormous and well-known companies such as Hilton Hotels and Harrah's and are now watching some of those companies teeter on the brink of insolvency; the compensation of the hedge fund managers who, despite losing 20 or 30 or

40 percent of their clients' money in one year, made tens of millions in years past, notwithstanding an ultimate track record that left many of their longtime investors lucky if they came out even.

They know there may be a pause in the obscene sums they were able to command. These are not stupid people. They sense the *zeitgeist*. But they also know that memories may be too short and the will of shareholders and limited partners too weak to deny them the riches they desire for too long.

Many of them are my friends. They are decent people. They are generous people. These are people who went to Wall Street because they knew that if they succeeded they would make a lot of money. And there is nothing wrong with that. But now they are complaining that they had nothing to do with causing this collapse and are still being held to account for it. And they are right; it doesn't seem completely fair. But the waiter who loses his job because the restaurant where he works serves awful food and closes as a result can say the same thing. Sometimes, that's just the way it is.

The toll for Americans of more modest means builds every day. Alan Greenspan told me the only thing he could have done to stop the housing bubble was to have raised interest rates so high that the housing bubble would have been decisively popped. "We could have clamped down on the American economy, generated a 10 percent unemployment rate and I will guarantee you we would not have had a housing boom, a stock market boom, or indeed a particularly good economy either," explained the former Fed chairman. Greenspan believes popping the housing bubble was an untenable solution that would have created an even bigger problem. But these days I find myself wondering whether that is true. Many expect the unemployment rate will exceed 10 percent sometime in 2009 or 2010.

Here in New York City, it is a strange time. There is foreboding. The restaurants are still often full and the streets still bustling. But there's a feeling in the air reminiscent of what it must have been like in Paris before the German army came storming in. We are all waiting for a change that seems inevitable given the carnage on Wall Street, the jobs and riches that have been washed away in the deluge of losses. No one is quite sure what that change will bring.

People who have no knowledge of what living in New York City during the 1970s was like, are nonetheless debating whether the city is headed into a similar era. It's a hot topic of discussion among the city's wealthy residents.

I grew up in New York City during the 1970s. I spent my childhood in Queens, and my years as an adolescent riding the New York City subway to and from my high school on the Upper West Side of Manhattan, a pretty long ride. I took it every day during the worst years this great city has ever seen to a neighborhood that was strewn with empty lots.

New York was a pretty sad place then. When I think back to that time, it always seems bathed in shades of grey. The city was dirty and somber and dangerous and seemingly empty. You could buy a four-bedroom apartment in Manhattan's best neighborhood for $80,000. But no one wanted to live in New York City then; it was only a place for those who couldn't get out. None of us stuck here could ever have imagined the tidal wave of Wall Street money that would transform the place where we lived in the decades to come.

I watched that money subsume the city I still live in. It has made it a far better place to raise a family and to work and live. The subway doesn't break down every day and Central Park could not be more beautiful. But I have never grown completely comfortable with it. I am not nostalgic for the 1970s. But I do remember a time when not everyone who lived in the borough of Manhattan was wealthy. I do remember a time when one might find friends who did something other than work at an investment bank, hedge fund, or private equity firm. And I do believe the city was a better place for it.

In the mid–1990s, I received my first invitation to an annual dinner that raises money for an organization called the Robin Hood Foundation. The foundation was started by a monumentally successful hedge fund manager named Paul Tudor Jones. Jones founded Robin Hood after the stock market crash of 1987. Its mission is to fight the effects of poverty in New York City and help build institutions that will reverse that poverty. It is a wonderful organization, run by a first-class staff and served by a board of directors who pay 100 percent of the foundation's annual operating expenses. Needless to say, most of the board derives its income from the financial services industry.

The fundraiser was held in an armory on Lexington Avenue and 26th Street. It was a large space. But there were few enough tables that an aggressive reporter might make his way around the venue during the night and meet and greet many of the attendees. Almost all of them were connected to the world of finance.

The evening included a live auction of some unique items—things like a hockey lesson for your kids taught by then–New York Rangers star Mark Messier or a private jet ride to Hollywood for a star-studded screening. I knew people on Wall Street made lots of money, but it was the first time I really stopped to consider just how much. I watched in awe as people I had never heard of made bids of two or three hundred thousand dollars on some of the items to be auctioned. Dozens of hands would still be in the air as the bids passed half a million dollars. Who were these people, I wondered.

In a few years, the annual fundraiser for the Robin Hood Foundation would outgrow the Lexington Avenue armory. It was moved to the biggest space its organizers could find on the island of Manhattan: the Jacob Javitz Convention Center. There was no longer even a hint of intimacy. To get up from one's table was to risk never finding your way back. Needless to say that with thousands of the richest people in the country in attendance, the dinner was by far the single largest fundraising event in the world. In 2007, the gala, attended by close to 4,000 people, raised $72 million in a single night. I find myself thinking about the Robin Hood gala these days. Will Robin Hood ever come close to raising that much money again? Will the annual dinner find itself bereft of attendees? What will that mean for all the good things this organization has done for New York?

But I also wonder, as painful a sign as it is, whether it marks the passing of an era best bid *adieu*.

Medical doctors became hedge fund managers and investment bankers. Engineers chose not to build or invent "physical things," but to devise complex securities such as CDOs. Computer scientists eschewed entrepreneurship for the chance to launch algorithms that would fuel winning investment strategies.

People bought homes they couldn't afford with mortgages they should never have been given. They refinanced perfectly sound loans with toxic muck so they could put in a new pool or a new kitchen. Wall Street was more than happy to give them the money.

Greed is the fuel that makes our capitalist system run. It is a powerful emotion. When I asked Alan Greenspan about it, he agreed, and then he gave me a sideways look from that famous 82-year-old face and said: "And you're going to outlaw that? Go ahead and try it."

A Note on Sources

Research for significant parts of this book originates with the work undertaken to report and produce the CNBC documentary, *House of Cards* (which first aired in February 2009). For that production, roughly 25 people, from homeowners and borrowers to Federal Reserve Chairman Alan Greenspan, were interviewed on camera. In addition to those people who are quoted in the book, I spoke to many others on background.

Data was used from the Federal Reserve, the U.S. Census Bureau, SEC filings from 1996 to 2009, as well as company reports and press releases of New Century, Merrill Lynch, First Franklin, and Lehman Brothers. I reference data and information from Inside Mortgage Finance, the Mortgage Bankers Association, the Federal Housing Administration, the House of Representatives Committee on Oversight and Government Reform, and the Home Mortgage Disclosure Act, among others.

Alan Greenspan's book, *The Age of Turbulence: Adventures in a New World* (New York: Penguin, 2007), and Phil Gramm's *Wall Street Journal* article, "Deregulation and the Financial Panic" (February 20, 2009) provided additional information.

Resources from CNBC

CNBC, first in business worldwide, offers a wide range of video, interviews, articles, timelines, and profiles on the companies and people involved in the ongoing economic crisis. For up-to-date information on the events impacting the world today, CNBC.com offers:

And Then the Roof Caved In

In-depth, behind the scenes information about the book and the crisis including web-only videos, interviews, and profiles (RoofCavedIn.cnbc.com).

House of Cards

Guide to the original CNBC documentary, in which David Faber reports on the origins of the global financial crisis, with exclusive clips from the program (HouseOfCards.cnbc.com).

Collapse of Bear Stearns

What many thought might be the worst of the financial crisis turned out to be only the beginning. An inside look at the brinkmanship that led to a new era in public-private crisis management and the demise of a legendary Wall Street firm (CollapseOfBearStearns.cnbc.com).

The Fall of Lehman Brothers

Many people thought federal regulators would help save this investment bank the way they had with Bear Stearns six months earlier, but Lehman's sudden failure cascaded through the global economy (FallOfLehman.cnbc.com).

Fannie & Freddie Takeover

The two government-sponsored lenders, Fannie Mae and Freddie Mac, are taken over by the federal government before they collapse under the weight of the mortgage mess (FannieAndFreddie.cnbc.com).

Struggle at AIG

Tens of billions of dollars in federal aid kept the giant insurer from failing, but its rescue remains controversial to this day, as questions about its operations and executive compensation dog the firm (StruggleAtAIG.cnbc.com).

Year on the Brink 2008

A special report on a one-of-a-kind year of firsts, including a stock market meltdown, crude oil's record rise and fall, trillions of dollars in wealth lost, the government's historic $700 billion bailout of America's financial system, and the election of the nation's first African-American president, who vowed to make sure such a collapse never happens again (YearOnTheBrink.cnbc.com).

Wall Street in Crisis

The casualties on Wall Street, from Bear Stearns to Lehman Brothers to Merrill Lynch to AIG—and the government's efforts to bailout the financial sector (WallStreetInCrisis.cnbc.com).

Greenspan: Power, Money & the American Dream

CNBC's extensive one-on-one interview with the nation's second-longest serving Federal Reserve Chairman Alan Greenspan and his recollections of such big events as the market crash of 1987 and the terror attacks of 2001 (Greenspan.cnbc.com).

Remembering the Crash of '87

Before the mortgage meltdown or the credit crunch came the grand-daddy of modern financial crises—the sudden and stunning stock market crash of 22 years ago. A look back at Black Monday, October 19, 1987, through the eyes of key players who were there (CrashOf87.cnbc.com).

Index